Reading Study Guide with Additional Support

UNITS 1-9

McDougal Littell

NORTH CAROLINA

in the American Experience

McDougal Littell

A DIVISION OF HOUGHTON MIFFLIN COMPANY

Evanston, Illinois • Boston • Dallas

ISBN10: 0–618–92449–3

ISBN13: 978-0-618-92449-3

2 3 4 5 6 7 8 9 - MJT - 12 11 10 09 08

Contents

How to Use this
Reading Study Guide with Additional Support

The purpose of this *Reading Study Guide with Additional Support*
is to help you read and understand your history textbook, *North
Carolina in the American Experience.*

Strategy: Read *Before, You Learned*
to review the main idea of the previous
section. Read *Now You Will Learn* to
get an overview of the current section.

Strategy: Read the Terms & Names.
Use the definitions to help you
understand the meaning of terms and
the significance of historical people.

Strategy: Fill in the diagram as
you read. The diagram will help you
organize information in the section.

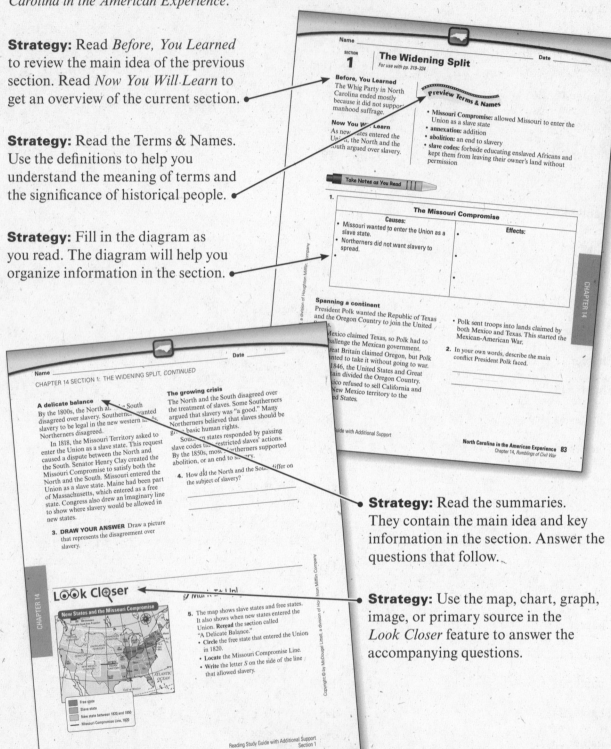

Strategy: Read the summaries.
They contain the main idea and key
information in the section. Answer the
questions that follow.

Strategy: Use the map, chart, graph,
image, or primary source in the
Look Closer feature to answer the
accompanying questions.

Name _____ Date _____

SECTION 1

North Carolina's Land Regions
For use with pp. 7–10

Before, You Learned
The five themes of geography are location, place, region, movement, and human-environment interaction.

Now You Will Learn
Geography played a key role as people decided where to settle and how to support themselves.

Preview Terms & Names

- **geographic region:** large land area with similar features
- **Coastal Plain:** broad, flat inland region along the coast
- **Piedmont:** hilly inland area with elevations from 500 to 1,500 feet
- **fall line:** dividing line between the Piedmont and the Coastal Plain

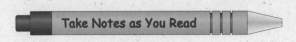
Take Notes as You Read

1.

North Carolina's Land		
Coastal Plain	**Piedmont**	**Mountains**
The land is flat and swampy along the east coast.	The land is	The land is

Regions of North Carolina

The physical terrain in North Carolina, called its topography, is divided into three regions. A geographic region is a large area of land with similar features. The three regions are

- the Coastal Plain
- the Piedmont
- the Mountains

"Coming unglued"

The east coast of North Carolina is home to the long chain of sandy islands called the Outer Banks. At some locations, points of land jut out into the ocean. These are known as capes.

Heading inland to the Coastal Plain

Several large bodies of water separate the Outer Banks from the mainland. Running inland for 100–150 miles from the ocean is a broad, flat region called the Coastal Plain. This area has many swamps, lakes, and rivers. Because it is so low, waters near the mouths of rivers rise and fall with the ocean tides. As a result, this area is known as the Tidewater, or Tidelands.

2. Explain one difference between the Outer Banks and the Coastal Plain.

_____

_____

The Piedmont

Farther inland, the land rises into gently rolling hills. This marks the start of the Piedmont, a region with elevations from 500 feet in the east to 1500 feet in the west.

Rivers and streams in the Piedmont often flow through deep cuts in the soil. In some places where the Piedmont meets the Coastal Plain, the change in elevation causes rocky rapids or waterfalls. This dividing line is known as the fall line.

3. DRAW YOUR ANSWER Draw a picture that shows the Coastal Plain, the Piedmont, and a river crossing the fall line.

The Mountains

At the western edge of the Piedmont are the Appalachian Mountains.

- These mountains run for 2,000 miles down the eastern coast of North America.
- Hernando de Soto named the mountains after the Apalachee, a group of Native Americans along Florida's Gulf Coast.
- North Carolina's Mt. Mitchell, in the Appalachians, is the highest mountain east of the Mississippi River.
- North Carolina may have the oldest mountains in the world.

4. In your own words, explain two special features of mountains in North Carolina.

_____

_____

LOOk Closer

Mark It Up!

5. This map shows the three geographic regions in North Carolina. It also shows the elevations in each area.
- **Circle** the name of the region that contains capes.
- **Locate** the area known as the fall line. **Draw** this line on the map.
- **Underline** the name of the region that contains Mt. Mitchell.

SECTION 2
North Carolina's Climate and Weather
For use with pp. 11–14

Before, You Learned
Geography played a key role as people decided where to settle and how to support themselves.

Now You Will Learn
North Carolina's climate is affected by its location, altitude, precipitation, and winds.

Preview Terms & Names

- **climate:** the main kind of weather that a region has over a long period of time
- **Sun Belt:** a strip of warm-weather states that runs across the southern United States

---

Take Notes as You Read

1.

North Carolina's Climate

Coastal Plain	Piedmont	Mountains
Temperature:	Temperature: cooler than Coastal Plain and warmer than Mountains	Temperature:
Precipitation:	Precipitation:	Precipitation:

North Carolina's Climate

Climate is the main kind of weather that a region has over a long period of time. North Carolina is located in the Sun Belt.

Location

A region's location affects its climate. Because North Carolina is closer to the equator, it is warmer than areas in the North. It has moderate year-round temperatures. With a long growing season, it is an ideal place for agriculture. Climate is also affected by a region's relationship to other natural features. North Carolina borders the Atlantic Ocean, so its climate is warm and moist.

Altitude

Air cools as it rises, so areas with higher elevations have cooler air. In North Carolina, the temperature along the east coast is much warmer than in the western mountains. The mountains also block cold air from the interior. Mountains do not block winds from the Gulf of Mexico or the tropical Atlantic Ocean.

2. Why does North Carolina tend to be warm year-round?

_____

_____

CHAPTER 1

Precipitation

Precipitation can come as rain, sleet, hail, snow, fog, or dew, depending on the temperature. North Carolina receives

- snow that can be heavy in the mountains.
- the most rain in July and August, and the least rain in October and November.
- thunderstorms during the hot months in Mountains and Coastal Plain.
- occasional hurricanes in the fall or violent winter storms called Nor'easters.

3. DRAW YOUR ANSWER Draw a symbol that shows the precipitation North Carolina usually has in the summer months.

Winds

For most of the year, winds blow into North Carolina from the southwest. In September and October, they come from the northeast. The wind is stronger on the coast than in inland areas.

- Winds can change direction suddenly, which can be dangerous for ships.
- Windmills have been used to power mills and wells, and to generate electricity.
- Winds reshape the sandy coastline. Grasses and fences are used to hold the sand in place.

4. In your own words, explain two ways that wind affects the coast of North Carolina.

_____

_____

LOOk Cl⊕ser

June 21 | December 22

✎ Mark It Up!

5. The left side of the diagram shows where the sun's rays hit the earth in June. The right side shows where the sun's rays hit in December.
   - **Reread** the section titled "Location."
   - **Circle** the name of the area on the diagram that has the warmest weather.

- **Locate** North America on both sides of the diagram. **Mark** it with the letter *N.*
- **Underline** the name of the month when North Carolina has its hottest weather.

SECTION
3

North Carolina's Natural Resources
For use with pp. 15–17

CHAPTER 1

Before, You Learned
North Carolina's climate is affected by its location, altitude, precipitation, and winds.

Now You Will Learn
North Carolina's resources include its soil, rocks, minerals, plants, wildlife, and water.

Preview Terms & Names

- **environment:** all the living and nonliving things that make up a region
- **natural resource:** the parts of nature that people use in some way
- **loam:** mixture of clay, sand, and decaying plants that is good for growing crops

Take Notes as You Read

1.

North Carolina's Natural Resources		
Coastal Plain	**Piedmont**	**Mountains**
•	•	•
•	•	• gems such as rubies and sapphires
•	•	•

Environment and Natural Resources
A region's environment is made up of living and nonliving things, including natural resources.

Soil
Soil is made up of rock particles and the remains of plants and animals that are broken down by heat, cold, rain, and wind. The soil in North Carolina varies.

- Coastal Plain: poor drainage in the Tidelands causes silt and muck to fill the marshes, but in the rest of the area, thick black loam is good for farming
- Piedmont: rocky, less-fertile soil that is difficult to farm

- Mountains: thinnest, rockiest soil in the state but trees grow well there

Rocks and minerals
North Carolina has at least 300 types of rocks and minerals. In the east: clay, sand, gravel, phosphate rock and peat; also lime along the coast; in the Piedmont: slate, granite, copper, and iron; in the Mountains: marble, limestone, talc, and gemstones

2. Explain one challenge of working with the rocky soil in the Piedmont.

_____

_____

Plants and wildlife

North Carolina has an amazing variety of plants and wildlife. Early settlers marveled at the buffalo and the large forests. Of all the plants, trees are the most important to the state's economy. Forests cover about 60 percent of all the land. North Carolina is the nation's leading producer of wooden furniture.

North Carolina is also home to a wide variety of wildlife, including black bears, deer, opossums, rabbits, wildcats, and many types of birds.

3. Why are trees important to North Carolina's economy?

_____

_____

_____

Water—offshore and inland

North Carolina's offshore waters are a valuable resource for many types of fish, such as channel bass, tuna, and blue marlin. North Carolina also has vast inland water resources. Its many rivers have helped move people and goods from place to place. Lakes contain fresh water, one of the world's most valuable resources.

4. DRAW YOUR ANSWER Draw a picture that represents the wildlife of North Carolina.

LOOk Closer

The thing I remember most about North Carolina are the flowers. The spring seemed to be filled with color. There were dogwoods, rhododendrons, and azaleas. Papa used to drive us to the mountains to see them. It was quite a display.

Haroldine Gold, a former resident of North Carolina

Mark It Up!

5. Read the primary source quotation.
- **Circle** the season described in the quotation.
- **Underline** the name of the geographic region described in the quotation.
- **Write** one sentence that summarizes Gold's memory of North Carolina.

_____

_____

SECTION
1

The First People of North America

For use with pages 23–27

Before, You Learned

Geography and climate affect where people settle and how they are able to live.

Now You Will Learn

Native people used available natural resources to build homes and provide food. This is why cultures varied from place to place.

Preview Terms & Names

- **Christopher Columbus:** sailed to Bahamas from Spain in 1492
- **culture:** a people's way of life
- **culture region:** area where methods of living are alike
- **mesa:** a high plateau
- **pueblo:** Spanish term for "town"
- **slash-and-burn:** method for clearing land

Take Notes as You Read

1.

Characteristics of Native American Cultural Regions		
Pacific Northwest	**Desert Southwest**	**The Plains**
People lived by fishing in oceans and rivers and by hunting whales.	People lived by	People lived by

Native American cultures

Long before Christopher Columbus landed in the Bahamas, Native Americans had many different cultures, or ways of life. Scientists group them into culture regions, areas where methods of living are alike.

The Pacific Northwest

The first fishing-whaling people arrived in the Pacific Northwest 7,000 to 9,000 years ago. Their descendents were the Makah.

The Makah

- ate fish from the oceans and rivers, and plants and game from forests.
- made canoes and huts from cedar planks.
- made rope, blankets, and clothing from cedar bark.
- using canoes they hunted whales, which meant extra food and oil for trade.

2. In your own words, explain how the Makah used the ocean as a natural resource.

_____

_____

_____

CHAPTER 2

CHAPTER 2

The Desert Southwest

The Hohokam, or "Perished Ones," settled the American Southwest about 2,100 years ago. They dug irrigation ditches to rivers to find water to grow gardens in the dry, dusty desert soil.

The Anasazi, or "Ancient Ones," moved into this region around the same time. They built huge apartment-like complexes out of sun-dried clay bricks called adobe. For protection, they settled in canyons and on the tops of high plateaus called mesas.

By the time the Spaniards arrived, the Hohokam and Anasazi had deserted their fields and towns. Other desert peoples farmed the dry land and built adobe villages that the Spaniards called pueblos, the Spanish term for "towns."

3. DRAW YOUR ANSWER Draw a picture that shows the homes built by the Anasazi.

The Plains

Another culture region formed on the grasslands of the Great Plains. This region had few trees and little water, and was populated by huge herds of buffalo. The people of the Plains used the buffalo in many ways and followed their migration.

- They used the meat for food and skins for clothes and shelter.
- They used the bones for tools.

The Eastern Woodlands

In the Eastern Woodlands, people hunted and farmed. They cleared land using the slash-and-burn method. Women planted seeds in the ashes. When the soil wore out, people moved on. Gradually new trees and plants grew.

4. Explain a difference between the Plains and Eastern Woodlands cultures.

_____

_____

_____

LO̲O̲k Cl⊕ser

Selected North American Cultural Groups, c. 1600

Haida
Kwakiuti
Chinook
Nez Perce
Blackfoot
Crow
Mandan
Cree
Ojibwa
Ottawa
Algonquin
Huron
Pomo
Shoshone
Cheyenne
(Sioux)
Dakota
Sauk
Potawatomi
Iowa
Miami
Shawnee
Iroquois
Wampanoag
Pequot
Delaware
Susquehanna
Paiute
Arapaho
Pawnee
Kansas
Kiowa
Osage
Chickasaw
Powhatan
Tuscarora
Chumash
Hopi
Navajo
Zuni
Apache
Cherokee
Pima
Pueblo
Comanche
Choctaw
Creek
ATLANTIC OCEAN
Seminole
PACIFIC OCEAN
Gulf of Mexico
Huichol
Aztec
Taino

0   40   80 miles
0   40   80 kilometers
Azimuthal Equal-Area Projection

Subarctic
Northwest Coast
California
Plateau
Great Basin
Mesoamerican
Southwest
Plains
Eastern Woodlands
Southeastern
Caribbean

✎ Mark It Up!

5. This map shows the cultural regions and first people of North America.

- **Locate** the four cultural regions discussed in this section.
- **Circle** the region that depended on fishing and whaling.
- **Write** the letter *B* on the region that depended on buffalo.

Copyright © by McDougal Littell, a division of Houghton Mifflin Company

SECTION 2

The First North Carolinians

For use with pages 30–33

Before, You Learned
Native Americans used available natural resources to live. This is why cultures varied from place to place.

Now You Will Learn
Artifacts and oral histories show how the first people in North Carolina lived and how they used natural resources.

Preview Terms & Names

- **oral history:** a story passed down from generation to generation
- **clan:** group of related people
- **anthropologist:** scientist who studies human culture

Take Notes as You Read

1.

Characteristics of Eastern Woodlands Cultural Region		
1	**2**	**3**
People used the slash-and-burn method to clear land for farming.		

Early groups in North Carolina

People have lived in North Carolina for over 10,000 years. The first people wandered the land and hunted. About 2,500 years ago they developed agriculture and began settling in villages. They developed many crafts such as pottery and jewelry making.

But the people did not leave written records. We can learn about them through the objects they left behind and through oral histories, stories passed down from generation to generation.

In 1492, about 35,000 Native Americans lived in North Carolina. The five largest groups were the Hatteras, the Chowanoc, the Tuscarora, the Catawba, and the Cherokee.

Europeans admired the endurance and strength of these peoples. Europeans noticed that Native Americans had darker skin, wore less clothing, and decorated their bodies with tattoos. Europeans seemed just as oddly clothed and dressed to the Native Americans.

2. In your own words, explain two ways we can learn about the first North Carolinians.

_____

_____

Leaving a mark on the land

The native peoples from the Outer Banks to the Appalachians used whatever the land offered.

- Coastal Plain: They turned the sandy loam into gardens.
- Tidewater: They made canoes and huts from cypress trees.
- The Piedmont: They caught fish along the fall line and used the slash-and-burn method to create fields for farming.
- The Mountains: They collected minerals such as quartz and mica.

3. DRAW YOUR ANSWER Draw a picture that shows how native peoples used the land in the Piedmont.

Patterns of life

Most native people in North Carolina shared certain cultural traits.

- The extended family was the basis of life.
- They traced ancestry through women.
- Clans, or groups of related people, lived in settlements of 10 or 12 houses.
- Each clan was ruled by a chief.
- They viewed life as a connection between humans, plants, and animals.

It took non-Native Americans a long time to understand the way Native Americans viewed the world. One of the first to study this was James Mooney, an anthropologist, or scientist who studies human culture.

4. In your own words, explain the role women played in the history of Native American clans.

_____

_____

L👓k Cl⊕ser

PRIMARY SOURCE

When the Plants, who were friendly to Man, heard what had been done by the animals, they determined to defeat the latter's evil designs. Each Tree, Shrub, and Herb, down even to the Grasses and Mosses, agreed to furnish a cure for some one of the diseases named, and each said: "I shall appear to help Man when he calls upon me in his need." Thus came medicine. . . . When the doctor does not know what medicine to use for a sick man, the spirit of the plant tells him.

Swimmer, *The Sacred Formulas of the Cherokees*

✎ Mark It Up!

5. **Read** the legend from the primary source.
   - **Circle** one word in the first sentence that describes the plants in the legend.
   - **Underline** the words said by each of the plants in the legend.
   - **Explain** how a doctor should choose medicine for a sick person, according to this legend.

_____

_____

SECTION 1

European Exploration of North America
For use with pages 41–47

Before, You Learned
Native Americans had different cultures.

Now You Will Learn
European explorers came to the Americas for various reasons.

Preview Terms & Names

- **conquistador:** Spanish adventurer
- **missionaries:** people who teach their religion to people of other faiths
- **mission:** a missionary settlement

Take Notes as You Read

1.

Economics		Religion	
Causes: Conquistadors such as Cortés and Pizarro wanted to become wealthy.	**Effects:**	**Causes:** The Catholic Church wanted to spread its faith to the Americas.	**Effects:**

Dividing the world
Spain and Portugal signed the Treaty of Tordesillas in 1494. The treaty created an imaginary line through the Atlantic Ocean. Spain could claim land west of the line, and Portugal could claim land to the east.

Spain builds an empire
Columbus established Spain's first settlements on the Caribbean islands. Soon, other Spanish adventurers called conquistadors followed him. They wanted wealth, adventure, and glory.

Cortés conquers Mexico; Pizarro conquers Peru
By 1521, Hernándo Cortés and his men had conquered the Aztecs in Mexico in 1532. The Spanish were determined to convert all Native Americans to Christianity.

Francisco Pizarro and his men reached the Inca Empire in 1532. Over the next 100 years, the Spanish conquered all of Peru whose metal mines made Spain rich.

2. Explain the main goals of the conquistadors.

_____

_____

CHAPTER 3

Missionaries spread Catholicism

In the 1500s, the Spanish monarchs sent Catholic priests to the Americas as missionaries, people who teach their religion to people of other faiths. They built small settlements called missions, and many used Native Americans as laborers. Millions of Native Americans died from diseases brought over by the Europeans.

The slave trade begins

During the 1500s, the Spanish and the Portuguese began buying slaves from African chiefs and shipping them to the Americas, where they replaced Native Americans as laborers.

3. **DRAW YOUR ANSWER** Draw a picture that shows the purpose of a missionary.

The Columbian Exchange

The arrival of the Spanish in the Americas caused a movement of plants, animals, and diseases known as the Columbian Exchange. More than 20 million Native Americans were killed by diseases. Europe and the Americas benefited from blending crops, livestock, and cultures.

Verrazano seeks a northwest passage

In 1524, Giovanni da Verrazano sailed to the Outer Banks. He was the first explorer to visit North Carolina. He believed he had found a northwest passage, a direct sea route to Asia. Verrazano then sailed farther north. He traveled as far as Newfoundland in Canada before returning to France. His reports helped France later claim lands in the New World.

4. Why did Verrazano sail to the Americas?

_____

_____

LO‍‍k Cl‍ser

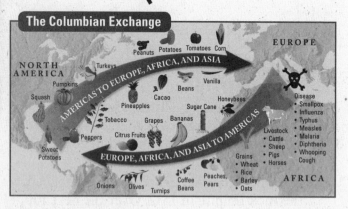

The Columbian Exchange

✐ Mark It Up!

5. This map shows the foods, animals, and diseases that passed between Europe, Asia, Africa, and the Americas.
   • **Locate** North America, Europe, and Africa on the map.

   • **Circle** one harmful thing brought to the Americas.
   • **Underline** one helpful thing brought from the Americas.

12 **North Carolina in the American Experience**
Chapter 3, *European Exploration of North America and North Carolina*

Reading Study Guide with Additional Support
Section 1

CHAPTER 3

SECTION 2

Europeans Reach North Carolina

For use with pages 48–53

Before, You Learned

European explorers came to the Americas for economic, political, geographic, and religious reasons.

Now You Will Learn

Spain's adventurers started colonies in the Americas.

Preview Terms & Names

- **Juan Ponce de León:** explored Florida for Spain
- **Lucas Vásquez de Ayllón:** tried to establish a settlement in North Carolina
- **Jean Ribaut:** led the first French expedition to the Americas

---

Take Notes as You Read

1.

Politics		Geography	
Causes: France decides to challenge Spain for land in North America.	**Effects:**	**Causes:**	**Effects:** Ponce de León explores Florida twice and claims land for Spain.

CHAPTER 3

Ponce de León claims Florida for Spain

Juan Ponce de León sailed to the Americas in 1513 hoping to find a fountain of youth. He named the region where he landed Florida, or "Feast of Flowers." Ponce de León returned to Florida seven years later. He tried to establish a settlement but was driven out by Native Americans. His travels gave Spain a claim to the lands he explored.

2. Why do you think Ponce de León wanted to find the Fountain of Youth?

_____

_____

Vásquez de Ayllón's expeditions

In 1526, Lucas Vásquez de Ayllón led an expedition to settle North Carolina. He brought 500 men, women, and children with him. The group found their first site too swampy, so they moved south. The settlement failed due to disease, starvation, a slave revolt, and attacks by Native Americans.

3. Identify one similarity between Ponce de León and Vásquez de Ayllón.

_____

_____

De Soto reaches North Carolina and the Mississippi

In 1539, Hernando de Soto took a group of 600 men to the Americas to search for gold. They forced Native Americans to help them.

In early 1540, de Soto and his men entered North Carolina and traveled west where they enjoyed the hospitality of the Native Americans. In 1541, they reached the Mississippi River.

France challenges, but Spain wins control of Florida

In 1562, Jean Ribaut led a group of French Protestants to the Americas, but the colony failed. A second colony also failed because the colonists did not know how to hunt, fish, or farm. In 1565, Spain sent warships commanded by Pedro Menéndez to stop the French fleet before it could unload supplies. The French fled, and Menéndez established St. Augustine.

Expeditions in North Carolina

The Spanish king wanted to convert the Native Americans to Catholicism. Pedro de Coronas led soldiers and friars to Chesapeake Bay in 1566. They were held back by a hurricane, but claimed land for Spain in part of North Carolina. In 1566, Juan Pardo led an expedition to search for a land route to Spain's gold mines in Mexico. They were unsuccessful. Then in 1570, the Spanish established a mission in Chesapeake Bay, but its members were killed by Native Americans. After this, they gave up efforts to spread Christianity north of St. Augustine.

4. Why did Spain give up trying to settle the Americas north of Florida?

_____

_____

LOOk Cl⊕ser

PRIMARY SOURCE

Among my services I discovered, at my own expense, the Island of Florida . . . I intend to explore the coast of the said island and see whether it connects with [Cuba], or any other, and I shall endeavor to learn all I can. I shall set out to pursue my voyage in five or six days hence.

Ponce de León, *"Letter to King Charles V"*

✏ Mark It Up!

5. **Read** the primary source quotation.
   • **Circle** the name of person to whom this letter was written.
   • **Underline** Ponce de León's three goals for returning to Florida.

14 **North Carolina in the American Experience**
Chapter 3, *European Exploration of North America and North Carolina*

Reading Study Guide with Additional Support
Section 2

CHAPTER 3

SECTION 1 — The Amadas and Barlowe Expedition
For use with pages 59–61

Before, You Learned
Explorers came to the Americas for many reasons.

Now You Will Learn
To gain wealth and challenge Spain, England began to explore North America, take land in the queen's name, and start colonies.

Preview Terms & Names

- **sea dog:** sea captain who attacked Spanish ships
- **colony:** overseas settlement ruled by the home country
- **charter:** a legal document that grants permission to explore, settle, and govern land
- **Walter Raleigh:** sent explorers to North America
- **Amadas and Barlowe:** first Englishmen to set foot in what is now North Carolina

---

Take Notes as You Read

1.

Important Early Events in England's Explorations		
1558 A rivalry between England and Spain intensifies with Elizabeth I being named queen of England.	**1578**	**1584**

Early English colonies

In 1558, Elizabeth I became queen of England. This led to a rivalry between Spain and England for power. Some English sea captains, called sea dogs, raided Spanish treasure ships and attacked Spain's colonies in Central and South America.

Some English people thought North America was a good place for colonies, or overseas settlements ruled by the home country. They thought colonies would bring wealth to England. In 1578, Queen Elizabeth I granted a charter to Sir Humphrey Gilbert. This legal document gave permission to explore, settle, and govern land in North

America. Gilbert led an expedition to Newfoundland. Deciding it was too isolated, he returned to England. On the voyage, his ship was lost. His half-brother Walter Raleigh took up his quest. Raleigh sent explorers to North America to find the best place for a colony.

2. In your own words, explain two ways that England tried to increase its power.

_____

_____

CHAPTER 4

Amadas and Barlowe

Raleigh chose Philip Amadas and Arthur Barlowe to sail to North America. They were the first Englishmen to set foot in what is now North Carolina. They claimed the land for Elizabeth I. They also described the land as beautiful and full of wildlife.

A friendly welcome

Amadas and Barlowe were welcomed by Native Americans who traded with them and offered them food and shelter. After six weeks of exploring, Amadas and Barlowe returned to England. Two Native Americans, Manteo and Wanchese, went with them.

3. **DRAW YOUR ANSWER** Draw a picture that shows Native Americans welcoming Amadas and Barlowe.

Report to Raleigh

The expedition returned to England, and Barlowe gave Raleigh a positive report. It described natural resources and friendly native peoples. Queen Elizabeth I was given a document asking for her permission to establish colonies in North America.

Recognition from the queen

Queen Elizabeth I was so pleased with Raleigh's success that she knighted him. England's land in North America was named Virginia, to honor Elizabeth I, "The Virgin Queen." England looked forward to establishing colonies in North America.

4. In your own words, explain why the English believed North Carolina was a good place to establish colonies.

_____

_____

LOOk Cl+ser

PRIMARY SOURCE

We brought [a Native American] aboard the ships and gave him a shirt, a hat, and some other things and made him taste of our wine and our meat, which he liked very well. . . . He fell to fishing, and . . . divided his fish into two parts. . . . After he had requited [repaid us for] the former benefits received, he departed out of our sight.

Arthur Barlowe, *"Report to Raleigh"*

Mark It Up!

5. This quotation describes one of the first meetings between English explorers and Native Americans.
   • **Read** the primary source quotation.
   • **Circle** four things that the explorers gave to the Native American.
   • **Underline** what the Native American then gave to the explorers.

Why do you think these men greeted one another by giving gifts?

_____

_____

CHAPTER 4

SECTION
2   Ralph Lane Colony
For use with pages 62–65

Before, You Learned

To challenge Spain and gain wealth, England set its sights on establishing colonies in North America.

Now You Will Learn

England established its first North American colony on Roanoke Island, but the colonists did not stay long.

Preview Terms & Names

- **Richard Grenville:** commander of the fleet to Roanoke Island
- **Ralph Lane:** governor of Roanoke
- **Wingina:** Native American chief who threatened to murder Lane
- **Simon Fernándes:** piloted the fleet to Roanoke Island.

Take Notes as You Read

1.

Reasons Why the Ralph Lane Colony Failed	
Food and Supplies	**Leadership**
•	• Many colonists were unhappy with Ralph Lane as their leader.
•	•

Voyage of the Colonists

In 1585, Raleigh decided to send an expedition to Roanoke Island to set up a lasting settlement. He based his choice on the report of Amadas and Barlowe. The group of 107 men planned to make homes for their families, who would arrive later.

Sir Richard Grenville was the fleet's commander. When one ship ran aground on a sandbar near the Outer Banks, many of their supplies were lost or spoiled. Finally, the colonists arrived at Roanoke Island.

Roanoke Island

The colonists built Fort Raleigh on Roanoke Island. Ralph Lane became their governor. Grenville returned to England for badly-needed supplies. The colonists explored the region.

- Some searched for ports from which to capture Spanish ships.
- Others gathered information from Native Americans, made maps, and painted pictures of the region.

2. Why do you think the colonists made maps and painted pictures?

_____

_____

_____

CHAPTER 4

Trouble for the colonists

The colonists began to run out of food as winter approached. Grenville had not returned, and the colonists had not been able to plant any crops. Native Americans had little food to share.

Many colonists were unhappy with Lane's leadership. Lane became aggressive toward the Native Americans. Wingina, a new Roanoke chief, planned to murder the colonists. Having been warned, Lane led a surprise attack against Wingina, killing him and several other Native Americans.

3. **DRAW YOUR ANSWER** Draw a picture that shows one of the troubles faced by the Roanoke colonists.

Abandoning the colony

Sir Francis Drake landed in Roanoke in 1586 and offered to leave supplies. Before the colonists accepted, a fierce storm hit. Lane and the colonists returned to England with Drake. Grenville arrived a few days later and learned that the colonists had fled. He also left for England, leaving just 15 men behind.

Achievements of the colony

Lane brought three valuable products home from North America: tobacco, corn, and the marsh potato. The colonists also brought back their notes, drawings, and maps. Raleigh remained determined to establish an English colony in North America.

4. In your own words, explain two benefits of the Ralph Lane colony.

_____

_____

LOOk Cl⊕ser

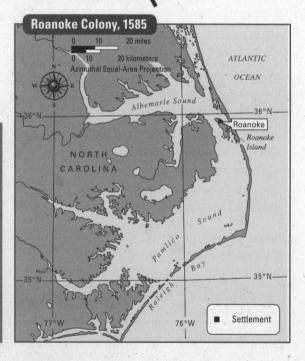

Roanoke Colony, 1585

✏ Mark It Up!

5. This map shows the coast of North Carolina and the location of Roanoke Island and the colonial settlement.
   • **Circle** Roanoke Island.
   • **Label** the chain of islands that includes Roanoke Island.

Why was it difficult for settlers to reach Roanoke Island?

_____

_____

CHAPTER 4

SECTION 3

The Lost Colony

For use with pages 66–69

Before, You Learned

England established its first North American colony on Roanoke Island, but the colony failed.

Now You Will Learn

England set up a second colony on Roanoke Island, which disappeared. No one knows what happened.

Preview Terms & Names

- **Croatoan:** friendly Native American tribe of which Manteo was a member
- **Lord of Roanoke:** title given to Manteo by England
- **Virginia Dare:** the first English child born in Virginia

Take Notes as You Read

1.

The John White Colony	
was formed because	**failed because**
• the first Roanoke colony had failed, and	•
•	•

The John White Colony

Raleigh decided to try again to set up a colony in North America. Its governor was John White.

The new colony was different. Women and children were among the 117 colonists. Men would be landholders. Raleigh chose Chesapeake Bay as the location because it could be reached more directly by sea.

The fleet's pilot refused to sail to Chesapeake Bay. He forced the colonists to land at Roanoke Island. They found few traces of the former colony.

Events at the colony

Soon a colonist was killed by Native Americans. Manteo, a member of the friendly Croatoan people, told the colonists that Wingina's men were responsible. For his loyalty, Manteo was given a noble's title.

Soon, the first English child was born in Virginia. She was named Virginia Dare. She was the granddaughter of John White.

2. In your own words, name two differences between the Roanoke colonies.

_____

_____

CHAPTER 4

White's departure in 1587

Like the colony before it, John White's colony quickly ran low on food. White sailed for England to gather supplies. The other leaders wanted to move the colony to a better site. They told White they would leave signs he could use to find them and also to let him know if they had been attacked.

When White reached England, his country was at war with Spain. All ships that could be used to defend England were forbidden to leave. White could not return to Roanoke for three more years.

3. **DRAW YOUR ANSWER** Draw a picture that shows why John White spent three years away from the Roanoke colony.

White's return in 1590

White found Roanoke deserted. He found carvings of the words CRO and CROATOAN, but no signs to show distress.

Searches for the Lost Colony

Bad weather prevented White from looking for the colonists. He never learned what happened to his colony.

Some historians think White's colony was destroyed by the Spanish or by Native Americans. Others think the colonists may have been lost at sea. Their fate remains a mystery.

4. Explain why White did not believe the colonists were in danger.

_____

_____

L👓k Cl🔍ser

[CRO] which letters presently we knew to signify the place, where I should find the planters seated, according to a secret token agreed upon between them & me at my last departure from them. . . . In Anno 1587 I willed them, that if they should happen to be distressed in any of those places, that then they should carve over the letters or name, a Crosse (+) in this forme, but we found no such signe of distresse.

Governor John White, *"Observations"*

🖉 Mark It Up!

5. This quotation describes signs that John White found carved on a tree and a post in the abandoned Roanoke settlement.
   • **Read** the primary source quotation.
   • **Underline** the three letters White found.
   • **Circle** the symbol that would have told White the colonists were in distress.

CHAPTER 4

Name _____ Date _____

SECTION 1

Jamestown and Economic Opportunity
For use with pages 75–78

Before, You Learned
In the late 1500s, the English made several unsuccessful attempts to establish permanent colonies in present-day North Carolina.

Now You Will Learn
Strict rules helped colonists eventually make Jamestown a successful British settlement.

Preview Terms & Names

- **John Smith:** Jamestown leader who worked to improve living conditions but then returned to England
- **apprentice:** people who learn a trade from skilled workers
- **House of Burgesses:** Jamestown's first government, composed of elected representatives

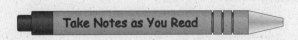

Take Notes as You Read

1.

Reasons for Settlement: Jamestown	
Causes	**Effects**
• Virginia Company hoped to gain wealth by finding gold.	• By 1608,
•	
•	• Because of strict rules about farming,

Planning a new colony
In 1606, King James I of England allowed the Virginia Company to build a colony in Virginia. The company hoped to gain wealth from the colony by finding gold, other natural resources, or a trade route to Asia. They also hoped to find out what happened to the Roanoke colonists.

Jamestown is settled
The colonists arrived in Virginia in April 1607, after a long and difficult journey. They named their settlement Jamestown. Jamestown was located on a river and was

protected by land on three sides. Virginia Company ships could reach it easily.

The new colony faces trouble
Life in Jamestown was harsh. All but 38 of the 144 colonists died in less than one year. The deaths were caused by diseases, starvation, and attacks by Native Americans who resented the colonists.

2. In your own words, explain two challenges faced by the Jamestown colonists.

_____

_____

Strong leaders emerge

By 1608, Jamestown was failing. Colonists faced starvation and some tried to return to England. John Smith forced colonists to plant crops, build, and trade with Native Americans, but he returned to England. Lord De La Warr forced colonists to farm, or face prison or death. Pocahontas, daughter of Native American chief Powhatan, married a colonist, leading to eight years of peace. During this time, tobacco became an important source of income for the colony.

3. **DRAW YOUR ANSWER** Draw a scene that shows how one leader tried to make life better for colonists in Jamestown.

New colonists and the first Africans arrive in Jamestown

By 1618, Jamestown needed more farm workers. Boys and girls came as apprentices to learn a trade from skilled workers. Jamestown also used indentured servants who worked in return for passage, clothing, and food. In 1619, 20 Africans were brought to Jamestown from the West Indies. They were eventually treated as slaves. White women also came to Jamestown. They married colonists and started families.

Colonists find a voice

In 1619, the Virginia Company allowed the colonists to elect their own leaders. These elected officials formed the House of Burgesses. It was modeled on the English Parliament.

4. What made Jamestown successful?

_____

_____

LO͡O͡k Cl⊕ser

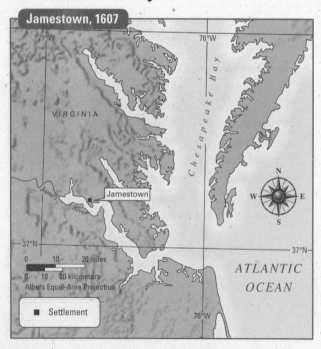

Jamestown, 1607

✎ Mark It Up!

5. This map shows the location of the Jamestown colony.
   - **Circle** the Jamestown settlement.
   - **Measure** about how many miles colonists traveled up the James River before settling at Jamestown. **Write** your answer.

   _____ miles
   - **Write** the letter *S* on the map where Spanish ships would sail.

Name _____ Date _____

Before, You Learned
Strict rules helped colonists eventually make Jamestown a successful settlement.

Now You Will Learn
Pilgrims and Puritans left England to establish colonies in North America. Religion played an important part in the colonies' laws and goals.

Preview Terms & Names

- **Puritan:** people who thought the Church of England needed to be "purified"
- **Separatist:** people who refused to accept the authority of the Church of England
- **Pilgrim:** name for the Separatists who sailed to North America
- **Mayflower Compact:** an agreement among Pilgrims

Take Notes as You Read

1.

Settlement of New England Colonies	
Causes	**Effects**
• Separatists wanted to leave England to set up their own churches. •	• •

Puritans and Separatists

In the 1600s, all English citizens had to obey the Church of England. Puritans thought the church needed to become less "Catholic." Separatists refused to accept the church's authority. Separatists decided to move to North America. They became known as Pilgrims, people who make a journey for religious purposes. They headed toward Virginia in 1620. They landed instead at Cape Cod in what is now Massachusetts.

Leaders sign the Mayflower Compact; Colonists meet Native Americans

The Pilgrim leaders signed the Mayflower Compact, an agreement to set up the colony's

government. They called their settlement Plymouth. Native Americans taught them how to grow food and hunt. They feasted with colonists to celebrate the first harvest.

The "great migration"

Puritans wanted to purify their faith and decided to send colonists to North America. Between 1630 and 1640, about 20,000 Puritans left England.

2. In your own words, explain why the Pilgrims came to North America.

_____

_____

_____

CHAPTER 5 SECTION 2: THE NEW ENGLAND COLONIES, *CONTINUED*

The Massachusetts Bay Colony

The Puritans settled on a harbor and called the settlement Boston. They were more educated, wealthier, and better prepared than the Pilgrims. They arrived in time to plant for the fall, and they had chosen John Winthrop as governor ahead of time.

Winthrop and the New England Way

The Puritans' colonies were built on hard work, education, and obedience to God. In 1691, they combined with Plymouth to form Massachusetts. Towns were made from congregations. Each town governed itself. All townspeople had to attend church services. Duty, godliness, hard work, and honesty became known as the "New England Way." Laws required that children learn to read so that everyone could read the Bible.

Intolerance leads to new colonies

Some Puritans questioned strict Puritan laws and left to set up new colonies. Rhode Island was formed around Portsmouth and Providence. Connecticut was founded by people who wanted men of all religions to be able to take part in government. New Hampshire became a separate colony.

Trade, slavery, and the Puritan Way ends

By 1700, New England merchants were trading lumber, furs, and fish with other countries. Ship captains tried to make a profit at each stop. Trade routes looked like triangles and this became known as triangular trade. New England's coastal towns began to grow. Puritan ministers warned against leaving God's path to pursue money, but their way of life was ending.

3. How do you think trade contributed to the growth of coastal towns?

_____

_____

LOOk Closer

PRIMARY SOURCE

So shall we keep the unity of spirit, in the bond of peace. . . . Ten of us will be able to resist a thousand of our enemies. . . . For we must consider that we shall be as a City upon a Hill, the eyes of all people are on us.

John Winthrop, *"Model of Christian Charity"*

✏ Mark It Up!

4. In this quotation, John Winthrop describes his beliefs about the Massachusetts Bay Colony.
   - **Read** the primary source quotation.
   - **Circle** two phrases that Winthrop uses to describe the colonists' relationships with one another.
   - **Underline** the phrase he uses to describe how the colony will appear to others.

SECTION
3
The Middle Colonies
For use with pages 88–91

CHAPTER 5

Before, You Learned

Pilgrims and Puritans left England to establish colonies for religious reasons.

Now You Will Learn

The English established colonies that offered religious tolerance and were successful in trade and industry.

Preview Terms & Names

- **Middle Colonies:** the colonies between Virginia and Massachusetts
- **Peter Stuyvesant:** Dutch governor of New Amsterdam
- **William Penn:** founder of Pennsylvania
- **Quaker:** religious sect also called the Society of Friends
- **surplus:** the amount that is more than what is needed

Take Notes as You Read

1.

Settlement of Middle Colonies	
Causes	**Effects**
• The English wanted New Amsterdam for themselves. •	• •

English, French, and Dutch settlers in North America

In the first half of the 1600s, the large territory between Virginia and Massachusetts had not been explored. In time, English settlers established the Middle Colonies (New York, New Jersey, Pennsylvania, and Delaware) there.

France and the Netherlands were also interested in settling North America.

- The French settled in what is now Canada.

- Henry Hudson sailed up the river now known as the Hudson and claimed land for the Netherlands.

New Amsterdam is established

The Dutch were interested in trade and making profits. They established the colony of New Amsterdam in the Hudson River valley. Fur trading was the colony's major source of profit. In 1626, the colony bought Manhattan Island and established the town of New Amsterdam. In 1664, the English took over the colony and renamed the town New York. Over time, England divided the land it owned into colonies.

2. Why did the Dutch want settlements in North America?

_____

_____

Copyright © by McDougal Littell, a division of Houghton Mifflin Company

New York is sparsely settled, but New Jersey grows quickly

Most people in New York lived near the mouth of the Hudson River. Northern and western New York had very few settlers, for four reasons: Dutch landowners would not sell land. Fur traders did not want farmers there. The French claimed much of the land. The Iroquois were willing to fight to keep settlers out.

The owners of New Jersey hoped to get rich from it. They sold land at low prices, promised religious freedom, and let colonists govern themselves.

3. DRAW YOUR ANSWER Draw a picture that compares the number of settlers in New York and New Jersey.

All faiths are accepted in Pennsylvania

William Penn, the founder of Pennsylvania, was a member of a religious sect called the Society of Friends, or Quakers. Quakers believed that all people were equal, and they had suffered in England. The king gave Penn land, and he planned a colony based on religious freedom. He designed the city of Philadelphia, which welcomed people of all faiths.

The Middle Colonies prosper

The Middle Colonies had rich resources and could easily trade with other colonies. Farmers produced lots of food and sold their surplus, or the amount that was more than they needed, at home and abroad. Trade and cities grew quickly.

4. Why did William Penn start a colony ?

_____

_____

LOOk Cl⊕ser

✎ Mark It Up!

5. This picture shows Philadelphia. The tower in the center is a church.
- **Circle** the church tower.
- **Why** do you think the church is in the center of the town?

_____

_____

- **Write** three words to describe how the city appears in the picture.

_____

_____

SECTION 4

The Southern Colonies

For use with pages 92–95

Before, You Learned
The English established colonies that offered religious tolerance and were successful in trade and industry.

Now You Will Learn
England slowly established colonies in the South. Farming was important to these colonies.

Preview Terms & Names

- **Southern Colonies:** Virginia, Maryland, North Carolina, South Carolina, and Georgia
- **plantation:** large farm on which crops are grown for sale; the people who raise the crops live on the farm
- **Middle Passage:** name given to the journey for slaves across the Atlantic Ocean

---

Take Notes as You Read

1.

Settlement of Southern Colonies	
Causes	**Effects**
• Maryland: Lord Baltimore wanted religious freedom for Catholics.	• Maryland:
• Carolina:	• Carolina:
• Georgia:	• Georgia: became a royal colony

Southern Colonies get started

Virginia was founded in 1607, but it was not until the 1630s that the next Southern Colony was founded. In the 1600s, Catholics could not worship freely in England and were not welcome in most of the colonies. In 1632, the king gave the land to start Maryland, a colony that would welcome Catholics.

Carolina was founded in 1663. Its owners hoped to gain wealth by selling land and collecting rent. However, colonists only settled in far northern and southern areas. In 1712, the colony split into North Carolina and South Carolina.

The last colony grows slowly

Georgia was started by a group of Englishmen who wanted to provide new lives for debtors, people who could not repay what they owed. They also wanted to stop Spain from settling north of Florida.

The colony grew slowly, and strict regulations caused farms to fail. It was attacked by both Spaniards and Native Americans. In 1752, its charter expired and Georgia became a royal colony.

2. How did Carolina and Georgia differ?

_____

_____

CHAPTER 5

Southerners lived off of the land

In the Southern Colonies, people farmed. They did not turn to city and town life, as in other colonies. On plantations, people lived and raised crops such as tobacco. The many harbors supported trade. Rivers ran far inland, so people could settle away from the coast.

Ways of life in North and South Carolina differed

North Carolina had few rivers and good harbors. As a result, most farms were small and people only raised enough food for themselves. The swamps in South Carolina were perfect for huge plantations that grew rice. Indigo was a major crop, too.

3. In your own words, explain one challenge faced by farmers in North Carolina.

_____

_____

Plantation owners and slaves lived very different lives

Plantation owners lived in great comfort. They decorated their homes with expensive goods, traveled widely, and wore the latest fashions.

Enslaved Africans had very different lives. They were sold to planters. They had poor food, poor clothing, and miserable housing. They worked long hours, and education was not allowed. The issue of slavery eventually led to the Civil War.

4. **DRAW YOUR ANSWER** Draw a picture that shows what life was like for plantation owners.

LO☉k Cl⊕ser

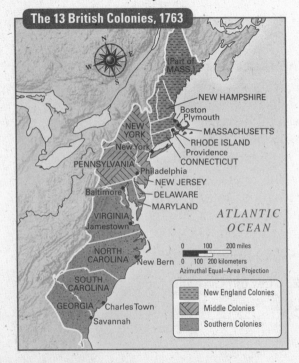

The 13 British Colonies, 1763

✎ Mark It Up!

5. This map shows the New England, Middle, and Southern colonies.
   - **Circle** the Southern Colonies on the map.
   - **Underline** the name of the smallest colony in the Southern Colonies.
   - **Measure** the distance in miles from Savannah to Boston. **Write** your answer.

   _____ miles

SECTION 1

A Proprietary Colony

For use with pages 103–107

Before, You Learned

England slowly established colonies south of Virginia.

Now You Will Learn

The owners of the land called Carolina wanted to gain wealth. They hoped settlers would arrive and governments could be put in place quickly.

Preview Terms & Names

- **naval stores:** products used in shipbuilding
- **Lords Proprietors:** owners and rulers of a tract of land given by the king
- **quitrent:** a land tax meant to cover the costs of governing a colony
- **prerogative party:** political party that wanted government to be independent of the people

Take Notes as You Read

1.

Sequence Events in North Carolina History		
1 1663: Charles II gives Carolina to Lords Proprietors.	**2**	**3**

Carolana

The Virginia Company's original charter included what is now North Carolina, but it was not settled. In 1622, John Pory explored the area. He found trees that were perfect for making ship masts and other naval stores, products used in shipbuilding. Native Americans in the area were eager to trade. They were already mining copper and gave some to Pory. His discovery made people interested in settling the area.

The Carolina colony changed hands several times in its early years.

- The Virginia Company lost its charter in 1624.

- King Charles I named the colony Carolana, the Latin form of *Charles*.
- Carolana became a colony in 1629, but it failed because no settlers arrived.
- Settlers from Virginia came in search of good land and adventure.
- By the early 1660s, as many as 500 people lived between Virginia and Albemarle Sound.

2. DRAW YOUR RESPONSE Draw a picture that shows naval stores.

CHAPTER 6

CHAPTER 6

The Lords Proprietors

In 1660, Charles II became king of England. He rewarded his supporters with land in Carolina. These eight men would be Lords Proprietors, or owners and rulers. Their colonists would have the same rights as Englishmen.

The first counties

The Proprietors divided Carolina into Albemarle, Clarendon, and Craven counties. They had several reasons for encouraging settlement. Settlers would provide goods and pay taxes. Also, land in Carolina could not be claimed by Virginia.

3. Explain why the Proprietors wanted to bring settlers to Carolina.

_____

_____

Government is established

The early government of Albemarle County had three parts:

- Assembly: elected delegates who controlled the colony's money
- governor: chosen by Proprietors and gave final approval on all laws
- Council: helped the governor make laws and acted as a court

A land tax called a quitrent helped cover the cost of running the government.

Political parties develop

Two political parties developed in Albemarle County. They disagreed about how the government should be run.

4. In your own words, explain the purpose of the Council.

_____

_____

LOOk Cl⊕ser

The Lords Proprietors of Carolina

Name	Position
Edward Hyde, Earl of Clarendon	Lawyer, member of Parliament, adviser to Charles I and Charles II, Lord High Chancellor of England
George Monck, Duke of Albemarle	Army general
William Craven, Earl of Craven	Army officer, friend of royal family
John Lord Berkeley	Fought for royal cause during civil war, joined royal family in exile
Anthony Ashley Cooper, later Earl of Shaftsbury	Chancellor of the Exchequer
Sir George Carteret	Naval officer, housed some of royal family at his home on the Isle of Jersey while they were in exile
Sir William Berkeley	Governor of Virginia at various times between 1641 and 1677, had knowledge of Carolina
Sir John Colleton	Planter on Barbados in the West Indies, had knowledge of Carolina

✏ Mark It Up!

5. This chart lists the Proprietors of the Carolina colony.
   - **Circle** the name of the Proprietor that was in charge of Clarendon County.
   - **Underline** the name of the Proprietor that served as governor of Virginia.
   - **Write** the names of two Proprietors that had knowledge of Carolina.

_____

_____

SECTION
2

First Settlers

For use with pages 108–111

Before, You Learned

The owners of the land called Carolina hoped settlers would arrive and governments could be put in place quickly.

Now You Will Learn

When a strong government was formed, Carolina grew rapidly.

Preview Terms & Names

- **Culpeper's Rebellion:** an uprising in which the popular party took over the North Carolina government
- **Seth Sothel:** corrupt leader who led Albemarle from 1683 to 1689
- **Philip Ludwell:** appointed governor of Albemarle in 1689
- **Gibbs's Rebellion:** John Gibbs's unsuccessful attempt to replace Ludwell as governor

CHAPTER 6

Take Notes as You Read

1.

Sequence Events in Carolina's Leadership		
1	**2**	**3** With Ludwell as governor, more settlers come to Carolina.

Growth goes slowly

The Lords Proprietors did not find gold in Carolina. To gain wealth, they tried to lure settlers from other colonies. Settlers were slow to come to Albemarle for many reasons. Forests and swamps made travel difficult. The waters were shallow, so only small boats could be used. Settlers were only allowed small land grants. Quitrents were higher than in Virginia.

Unpopular trade laws lead to rebellion

The Lords Proprietors did not establish a strong government for the colony. Some governors were weak or dishonest.

The Navigation Acts made the situation worse. These unpopular laws restricted trade in the colonies. Goods shipped between colonies were taxed by England. The Lords Proprietors enforced them because they did not want to lose their charter.

2. In your own words, explain one reason why the colonists disliked the Navigation Acts.

_____

_____

Two factions clash; Sothel is appointed

The popular party tried to prevent the Navigation Acts from being enforced. The prerogative party vowed to uphold the new laws.

- 1676: During Culpeper's Rebellion, the popular party took control of the government, leading it for two years.
- 1678: John Culpeper, went to England to meet with the Lords Proprietors. He was tried for treason but found not guilty.

The colonists chose Seth Sothel to be their next leader. On his way to Carolina, he was captured by pirates and imprisoned for several years. His corrupt rule lasted from 1683 to 1689.

3. In your own words, explain the cause of Culpeper's Rebellion.

_____

_____

Ludwell takes over; The colony expands

In 1689, the Proprietors named Philip Ludwell governor of Albemarle. Soon after he arrived, Captain John Gibbs declared himself governor. This was called Gibbs's Rebellion. The Proprietors supported Ludwell. Northern Carolina then had 15 years of peaceful, effective government under his rule.

In 1696, Bath County was established. With the area at peace, many settlers arrived, including French Huguenots hoping to find religious freedom. Protestant settlers came from Germany, Switzerland, and England. Albemarle's population grew from 4,000 in 1675 to 15,000 in 1710.

4. **DRAW YOUR ANSWER** Draw a "before and after" picture of Albemarle to show its change in population.

_____

LOOk Cl⊕ser

PRIMARY SOURCE

A Brief DESCRIPTION
OF
The Province
OF
CAROLINA
On the COASTS of FLOREDA.
AND
More perticularly of a *New-Plantation*
begun by the *ENGLISH* at *Cape-Feare*,
on that River now by them called *Charles-River*,
the 29ᵗʰ of *May*. 1664.

Wherein is set forth
The *Healthfulness* of the *Air*; the *Fertility* of
the *Earth*, and *Waters*; and the great *Pleasure* and
Profit will accrue to those that shall go thither to enjoy
the same.

Also,
Directions and advice to such as shall go thither whether
on their own accompts, or to serve under another.

Together with
A most accurate MAP of the whole *PROVINCE*.

London, Printed for *Robert Horne* in the first Court of *Gresham-
Colledge* neat *Bishopsgate street*. 1666.

✎ Mark It Up!

5. **Read** the primary source document.
   - **Underline** the specific location of the new settlement in Carolina.
   - **Circle** the section that lists the benefits of living in Carolina.
   - **Write** the letter *P* next to the city where the pamphlet was printed.

SECTION 3

North Carolina Is Formed
For use with pages 112–119

Before, You Learned
When a strong government was formed, Carolina grew rapidly.

Now You Will Learn
North Carolina split from South Carolina. Strong leadership helped the colony succeed. In time, it was sold back to the English Crown.

Preview Terms & Names

- **Dissenter:** person who opposed the Anglican Church
- **Henderson Walker:** governor who passed the Vestry Act
- **Vestry Act:** church law that called for parishes, vestries, and church buildings, and taxed colonists to support clergy
- **Edward Hyde:** first governor of North Carolina
- **borough town:** a town large enough to send delegates to Assembly

Take Notes as You Read

1.

Sequence Events in Carolina's Leadership		
1	**2**	**3** Seven of the eight Proprietors sell their shares to the Crown.

Colonists worship as they please; Anglicans try to take over; Quakers protest

The official church of Carolina was the Anglican Church. However, all Protestant groups worshiped freely. Dissenters such as the Quakers disagreed with the Anglican Church.

In 1699, Henderson Walker, an Anglican, became governor. He passed the Vestry Act, which called for building Anglican churches and created a tax to support clergymen. The Proprietors did not approve the act.

In 1703, a law was passed requiring that all Assemblymen be Anglicans and swear allegiance to the English queen. Quakers

protested and eventually the law was revoked. Many Quakers were elected to office.

Carolina becomes two colonies

The Proprietors separated the colony into North and South Carolina so the northern part could be better governed. On May 9, 1712, Edward Hyde became governor of North Carolina.

2. In your own words, explain why the colony was split into North and South Carolina.

_____

_____

Tuscaroras go to war; South Carolina helps; Good government prevails

Native Americans called Tuscaroras were upset at the colonists for many reasons, including the taking of their land. In September 1711, they attacked settlements.

South Carolina sent money and troops to help Governor Hyde. In time, colonists and Native American allies defeated the Tuscaroras, but the loss of life, livestock, and destruction of the land was vast. New colonists stayed away from North Carolina.

The Assembly fixed government problems and made the laws clearer. Borough towns were allowed to send a delegate to the Assembly. New laws encouraged business and improved travel. Channels were cleared, improving sea trade.

Pirates take to Carolina waters

The cleared channels attracted pirates, who stole goods from merchants. The most famous of these was Blackbeard. He and others were captured and killed.

The colony expands; The proprietors sell their shares

With the victory over the Tuscaroras, decreased threats from pirates, and strong leadership, North Carolina grew. Four new counties were added between 1722 and 1730; more settlers arrived. Even areas that had been abandoned earlier were settled.

As North Carolina flourished, England wanted it to be a royal colony. Surveyors firmly established North Carolina's boundaries. On July 25, 1729, the Proprietors sold the colony back to the English Crown.

3. List two challenges that North Carolina faced after splitting with South Carolina.

_____

_____

_____

LOOk Closer

✏ Mark It Up!

4. This painting shows a Quaker meeting.
   - **Circle** the person in the painting whose head is uncovered.
   - **Write** the letter *W* on each woman in the painting.
   - **Write** the letter *C* on each child in the painting.
   - How does the painting show that Quakers believed all people were equal?

_____

_____

SECTION 1 — Diverse Groups in the Colony
For use with pages 125–129

Before, You Learned
Strong leadership helped North Carolina succeed after it split from South Carolina.

Now You Will Learn
In the 1700s, new immigrants helped North Carolina thrive. Not everyone living there, however, benefited.

Preview Terms & Names

- **Highland Scots:** people from a part of Scotland
- **backcountry:** thinly populated settlements that stretched from the fall line to the Appalachians
- **Scots-Irish:** descendants of Scots in Ireland
- **Pennsylvania Dutch:** term for all German-speaking settlers, most of whom fled religious persecution in German states

Take Notes as You Read

1.

Group	Important Details
Highland Scots	Land:
Pennsylvania Dutch	Religion:
Native Americans	Cherokee Population:

Reasons for immigration
North Carolina's population grew in the mid-1700s. People read about the colony's mild climate, fertile soil, and inexpensive land. Some wanted to escape religious and political difficulties in Europe. Others wanted to leave behind crowded conditions or harsh landlords.

Moving into Cape Fear; Great Wagon Road
The Highland Scots were the first large immigrant group in North Carolina, whose governor was also a Scot. He helped Scots get land. Thousands more Highland Scots came after 1746, when the English stopped an uprising in Scotland and took the Highlanders' land. Many fled to Upper Cape Fear, where the population grew so large that the Assembly created a separate county in the region called Cumberland.

In the 1700s, a large number of settlers came from Pennsylvania. They created the Great Wagon Road along the base of the Appalachian Mountains.

The two main groups that settled in the backcountry were Scots-Irish and German-speaking Protestants.

2. In your own words, explain why Highland Scots came to North Carolina after 1746.

_____

_____

_____

Copyright © by McDougal Littell, a division of Houghton Mifflin Company

CHAPTER 7

The arrival of the Scots-Irish and the Pennsylvania Dutch

The Scots-Irish came to colonial America from Ireland at the encouragement of the British. They were descended from Scots who were sent to Ireland in the early 1600s. As a result, the Scots-Irish had no love for England. They valued independence, supporting colonial revolution against England in the 1770s.

German-speaking settlers were known as the Pennsylvania Dutch. Most were Protestants who came to America in search of religious freedom. Groups such as the Moravians formed close communities. Many continued to speak German into the 1840s.

3. **DRAW YOUR RESPONSE** Draw a picture that shows why the Pennsylvania Dutch came to America.

Slavery; Native Americans

North Carolina had fewer slaves than any other Southern colony. Lacking good ports, slave trade was not active. The colony's farms and plantations were smaller than those in other Southern colonies. Also, North Carolina's Quakers opposed slavery.

Native Americans struggled in North Carolina in the 1700s.

- Some colonists sold them into slavery.
- 1715: Several groups declared war on the colonists; they reached peace in 1721.
- 1738: Almost half the Cherokees were killed by smallpox.
- 1776: The Cherokee had been forced to give up more than half of their land.

4. Give two reasons why Native Americans struggled in North Carolina.

_____

_____

_____

LO◯k Cl⊕ser

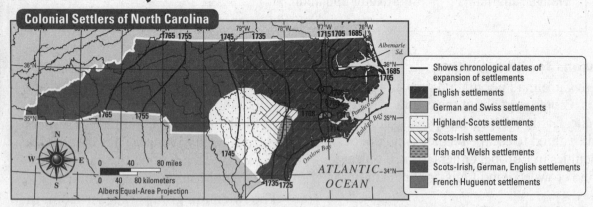

Colonial Settlers of North Carolina

Shows chronological dates of expansion of settlements
English settlements
German and Swiss settlements
Highland-Scots settlements
Scots-Irish settlements
Irish and Welsh settlements
Scots-Irish, German, English settlements
French Huguenot settlements

✐ Mark It Up!

5. This map shows when and where different groups of people settled North Carolina.
   - **Circle** the area settled by the Scots-Irish.
   - **Underline** the names of the four groups that settled North Carolina in and after 1725.

- When did Highland Scots settle North Carolina?

_____

_____

SECTION 2

Social Differences
For use with pages 130–133

Before, You Learned

In the 1700s, new immigrants helped North Carolina thrive.

Now You Will Learn

North Carolina developed a social structure that was more like England than New England and the Middle Colonies.

Preview Terms & Names

- **gentry:** people at the top of North Carolina society; they had some wealth and education
- **planters:** gentry whose wealth came from owning land and slaves; also called landed gentry
- **militia:** a force of volunteer soldiers
- **racism:** the belief by some that people of one race are superior to those of another

Take Notes as You Read

1.

SUMMARIZING

Group	Social ranking	How they lived
• Gentry	• the highest level	•
• Enslaved Africans	•	•

"Gentlefolk"

During colonial times, people were aware of social class and their position in society. In the backcountry of North Carolina, however, this was not true. In this region, people treated one another as equals.

In the mid-1700s, many people in the Coastal Plain tried to set up a social order like the one in England. At the top of society were the gentry—people with some wealth and education, such as doctors, clergy, and public officials.

The most important members of the gentry were the planters, or landed gentry. They had plantations, and they also owned shops, mills, or other services. Many were voted into public

office out of respect for their position in society. They enjoyed a life of comfort and luxury.

"A people very laborious"

In the early years of settlement, Englishman John Lawson had described North Carolinians as "a people very laborious." He noticed that people worked hard to improve their way of life. Lawrence Lee described North Carolina society as "elegant."

2. Describe those at the top level of North Carolina society in the mid-1700s.

_____

_____

CHAPTER 7

"Folks of a lesser sort"

Farmers and skilled tradesmen were the largest social group. Indentured servants signed contracts to work for others for a period of time. Apprentices worked in exchange for food, shelter, and instruction in a trade.

"Bonded for life"

At the bottom of colonial society were people "bonded for life," or enslaved Africans. Even free Africans had very low status as a result of racism, the belief that people of one race are superior to those of another. Enslaved Africans were considered property. Laws restricted their rights.

3. In your own words, explain why even free Africans had low status in North Carolina.

_____

_____

North Carolina: a "Southern" society

North Carolina's social structure was more like colonies in the South than colonies in the North.

- Geography: Tobacco and rice were easy to grow. This led farmers to build plantations.
- Slavery: Enslaved Africans worked on plantations. This deepened class differences.
- Lords Proprietors: The first owners of the colony were members of England's upper class. The government tried to create this same society in the colony.

4. **DRAW YOUR RESPONSE** Draw and label a symbol that represents North Carolina's social structure in the 1700s.

LOOk Cl⊕ser

PRIMARY SOURCE

Merchants in the town, and considerable planters in the country, are now beginning to have a taste for living. . . . They are generous, well bred, . . . polite, humane, and hospitable. . . . Their houses are elegant, their tables are always plentifully covered and their entertainment sumptuous. They are fond of company, living very sociable and neighbourly [lives], visiting one another often. Poverty is almost an entire stranger among them.

Lawrence Lee, *The Lower Cape Fear in Colonial Days*

✏ Mark It Up!

5. **Read** the primary source quotation.
- **Underline** the two social groups that Lee mentions in the first sentence.
- **Circle** three words that Lee uses to describe the people of North Carolina.
- **Which** specific settlement does Lee describe?

_____

_____

CHAPTER 7

SECTION 3 | The Products of Farm, Field, and Forest

For use with pages 134–135

Before, You Learned

North Carolina developed a social structure more like England's.

Now You Will Learn

During the 1700s, North Carolina developed an economy based on agriculture and trade.

Preview Terms & Names

- **cash crop:** crop sold for a profit
- **corduroy road:** a road formed by placing small tree trunks over a muddy path

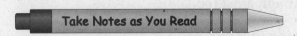

Take Notes as You Read

1.

SUMMARIZING		
Group	**Farming**	**Transportation**
Colonists	• They learned to farm from Native Americans. •	• • Most colonists traveled by river.

Nature's bounty

Because North Carolina has a mild climate, early settlers tried to grow warm-weather crops such as olives and lemons. When these crops failed, they grew staple crops such as wheat, oats, barley, and rye, which flourished.

They also grew Native American crops such as corn, tobacco, potatoes, squash, sunflowers, sweet potatoes, beans, and peas. Settlers learned to farm like Native Americans.

- They planted seeds in rows and hills.
- They cut weeds with wooden hoes.
- They used scarecrows to frighten away birds and other animals.

North Carolina farmers sold their goods in England, the West Indies, and New England. Corn, wheat, and tobacco were the most successful cash crops, or crops sold for a profit.

People used corn for cooking, making whiskey, and feeding livestock. Wheat sold especially well in England, where there was not enough land to grow the crop.

2. **DRAW YOUR ANSWER** Draw a picture that shows one of the Native American farming methods used by settlers.

CHAPTER 7

Nature's bounty, *continued*

Tobacco was one of the most successful nonfood crops grown in North Carolina. Farmers kept demand high by destroying low-quality plants and selling only those of the highest quality. Merchants came all the way from Scotland to purchase Carolina tobacco.

Other valuable products included:

- fruits and garden vegetables
- hogs and salt pork
- naval stores, products used for shipbuilding
- lumber and wood products such as shingles

3. In your own words, explain why tobacco farmers destroyed plants of low quality.

_____

_____

Bumping along the roads

Like other colonies, North Carolina had few good transportation routes. Most highways were muddy or filled with stumps. In some places, settlers laid small tree trunks across muddy roads to form what became known as corduroy roads.

Wealthy people had horse-drawn coaches, while others owned two-wheel carts. As the backcountry's population grew, so did the number of roads connecting east and west. This was a slow process, and rivers remained the main trade routes through most the 1700s.

4. In your own words, explain why most North Carolinians traveled by river during the 1700s.

_____

_____

LOOk Closer

✎ Mark It Up!

5. This picture shows three steps in the process of farming tobacco; planting, picking, and transporting.

- **Draw an arrow** to the person in the picture who is planting tobacco.
- **Circle** the three people in the picture who are picking tobacco.
- **Write** the letter *T* next to the two people who are preparing to transport the tobacco away from the field.

CHAPTER 7

SECTION 1

North Against South

For use with pages 141–144

Before, You Learned

During the 1700s, North Carolina developed an economy based on agriculture and trade.

Now You Will Learn

Regional differences affected the development of North Carolina's colonial government.

Preview Terms & Names

- **sectionalism:** strong loyalty to the region or section where a person lives
- **Granville District:** an area in northern North Carolina from which the Earl Granville collected taxes
- **quorum:** a majority of members
- **anarchy:** a complete absence of government
- **Arthur Dobbs:** became governor in 1752

Take Notes as You Read

1.

Main Idea	Summary of Details
Conflict grew between northern and southern counties.	Quitrents:
	Unequal representation in the Assembly:

The start of sectionalism

North Carolina did not have a permanent capital for nearly 40 years after it became a royal colony. The older counties in the north and the newer counties in the south could not compromise on a site for a capital. This led to sectionalism, or strong loyalty to the area or region where a person lives.

The Granville District

In 1729, Earl Granville refused to sell his share of the colony to the crown. He was entitled to one-eighth of all quitrents collected in North Carolina, South Carolina, and Georgia. King George II

ordered a survey, and the Granville District was created in northern North Carolina.

The creation of the Granville District led to conflicts. The Granville District had most of the colony's population and wealth. It also had many settlers who occupied land without paying for it. They did not want to pay quitrents. This angered settlers in the south.

2. **DRAW YOUR ANSWER** Draw a map showing the location of the Granville District.

CHAPTER 8

A challenge and a spokesperson for Cape Fear

Another source of conflict between northern and southern counties was unequal representation. The five old Albemarle counties each had five representatives in the Assembly. New counties in Cape Fear had only two representatives each. Governor Gabriel Johnston wanted to help the Cape Fear counties. He gathered the Assembly at Cape Fear when bad weather kept the delegates from Albemarle away. The Assembly met without a quorum, or a majority of members, present. They raised quitrents in the north to equal those in the south. They made New Bern the permanent capital, and they cut Albemarle's representatives to two per county.

3. Explain how Johnston helped Cape Fear.

_____

_____

Albemarle in revolt

The people of Albemarle called the Assembly a fraud and protested. They withdrew from the Assembly and even threatened to withdraw from the colony. For seven years, the north lived in anarchy, a complete absence of government. People refused to follow laws or pay taxes. The southern counties also refused to pay taxes.

Reunion

When Governor Johnston died, Arthur Dobbs replaced him. King George II ordered Dobbs to set aside the laws passed by the southern counties. The Albemarle counties once again sent five representatives each to the Assembly.

4. In your own words, explain why people in Albemarle refused to follow the laws passed by the southern counties.

_____

_____

LOOk Cl⊕ser

PRIMARY SOURCE

There is . . . in the older counties [Albemarle] a Perfect anarchy. As a result, crimes are of frequent occurrence, such as murder, robbery, etc. . . . The citizens do not appear as jurors, and if court is held to decide such criminal matters no one is present. If anyone is imprisoned, the prison is broken open and no justice administered. In short most matters are decided by blows.

August Spangenberg, *Records of the Moravians in North Carolina,* vol. 1

✎ Mark It Up!

5. **Read** the primary source quotation.
   - **Underline** counties Spangenberg describes.
   - **Circle** three problems he observed in these counties.
   - **What** happened to people put in prison?

_____

_____

CHAPTER 8

SECTION 2

East Against West

For use with pages 145–151

Before, You Learned
Regional differences affected North Carolina's colonial government.

Now You Will Learn
Differences in culture and disagreements over leadership increased tension between eastern and western counties.

Preview Terms & Names

- **barter system:** an exchange of goods and services
- **extortion:** illegal demands for fees
- **poll tax:** a tax on each individual
- **Regulator:** a member of a western group created to prevent abuses of power
- **Battle of Alamance:** fight between Tryon's troops and the Regulators

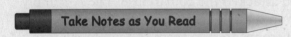

Take Notes as You Read

1.

Main Idea	Summary of Details
Conflict grew worse between eastern and western counties.	Representation in the Assembly:
	Public officials:

East and west develop different cultures and compete for representation in the Assembly

A governor's building project revealed a growing split between east and west. People in eastern North Carolina enjoyed the comforts of a civilized life. In the west, people were still settling the land. Their economy was based on the barter system. Each group disliked the other's way of life.

As the west grew, the government made new counties. However, it also added counties in the east so the east had more representatives in the Assembly.

Selection of officials angers the west

The organization of colonial government added to the conflict between east and west. The governor appointed easterners to county offices. Conflict between the westerners and these officials was common.

2. **DRAW YOUR ANSWER** Draw a picture that shows one difference between the eastern and western counties.

CHAPTER 8

Copyright © by McDougal Littell, a division of Houghton Mifflin Company

Westerners complain about officials; "Eastern ways" cause friction

Colonial county officials were allowed to charge fees for their services. These fees were set by the Assembly. Some officials in the backcountry were corrupt and greedy. They charged higher fees than they were allowed. If settlers could not pay their fees in the right currency, corrupt officials seized their land and sold it.

To westerners, public officials seemed selfish and unconcerned about the opinions or rights of the people. Many westerners complained about excessive taxes, dishonest officials, and extortion—illegal demands for fees. Their complaints were ignored.

3. In your own words, explain why westerners disliked their public officials.

_____

_____

_____

The cost of the governor's palace; The Regulator movement

In 1768, the dispute between east and west grew worse. A new poll tax to pay for the governor's palace was begun. Citizens in Orange County refused to pay the tax.

Leaders in Orange County established the Regulators. This group worked to prevent abuses of power. The Regulators challenged officials they believed to be corrupt. The Regulators charged one official, Edmund Fanning, with extortion. A court found him guilty but did not punish him. In response, a mob attacked the courthouse. The Assembly declared the Regulators to be outlaws and sent troops to stop them. A few Regulators were executed, but most were pardoned. The division between east and west remained.

4. In your own words, explain why the western mob attacked the courthouse.

_____

_____

_____

LOOk Clser

Mark It Up!

5. This picture shows Governor Tryon addressing a group of backcountry farmers.
- **Draw** an arrow to Governor Tryon.
- **Circle** the backcountry farmers.
- **Write** two words that describe Governor Tryon and his soldiers.

_____

_____

- **Write** two words that describe the backcountry farmers.

_____

_____

CHAPTER 8

SECTION

1

Orders from Abroad
For use with pages 159–161

Before, You Learned

Tensions developed between eastern and western counties in North Carolina.

Now You Will Learn

When North Carolina became a royal colony, its Assembly struggled, due to the new royal governor's instructions from England.

Preview Terms & Names

• **George Burrington:** the first royal governor of North Carolina

• **veto:** overrule a law

Take Notes as You Read

1.

Sequencing Events: George Burrington		
1729	**1730**	**1731**

Traveling Great Distances

In the early 1700s, mail service between the colonies and England was slow and unreliable. People with important business in England often traveled there rather than risk their letters getting lost along the way.

In 1729, George Burrington went to England to convince the Crown to name him the first royal governor of North Carolina. He was appointed governor in 1730, but he had to wait one year for his instructions. He would report directly to King George II of England rather than to a group of private Proprietors.

Defending the interests of empire

North Carolina was controlled by the English Board of Trade. To bind the colonies and England into one empire, the Crown appointed all royal governors and judges in the colonies. As royal governor, Burrington could veto, or overrule, colonial laws, and enforce the Navigation Acts, forcing colonists to support English shipping.

2. Why did England appoint royal officials?

_____

_____

_____

Defending the interests of the people

England assumed that it had control over the colonies, but the people of North Carolina had other ideas. The Proprietors had always allowed the colonies to handle their own affairs. When Burrington tried to exert his power over the Assembly, it responded with anger.

In 1731, Burrington sent a report to England. He explained that a governor could not flatter or trick the people of North Carolina. North Carolinians tended to disobey the orders given by their governors. Previous governors had also been unsuccessful.

3. Explain why Governor Burrington had trouble establishing his authority.

_____

_____

North Carolina experienced ongoing conflict between the Assembly and the royal governor until the American Revolution. Both sides disagreed about the role of the colonial assemblies. The people of North Carolina believed that the assemblies should represent the wishes of the colonists. Most English officials believed that the assemblies should carry out orders from England. This conflict eventually caused all thirteen colonies to unite against England.

4. DRAW YOUR ANSWER Draw a picture that shows how North Carolinians viewed their Assembly.

LOOk Cl⊕ser

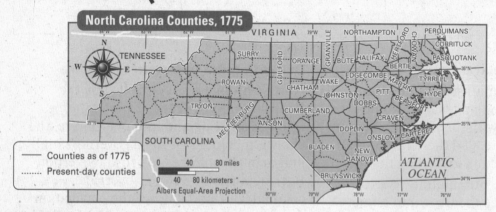

North Carolina Counties, 1775

—— Counties as of 1775
········ Present-day counties

0   40   80 miles
0   40   80 kilometers
Albers Equal-Area Projection

✎ Mark It Up!

5. This map shows the counties in North Carolina in 1775 and in the present day.
- **Circle** the part of the state that had the fewest counties in 1775.
- **Underline** the names of the counties that border South Carolina.

- **Why** do you think the number of counties in North Carolina has increased since 1775?

_____

_____

SECTION 2 — The French and Indian War

For use with pages 162–166

Before, You Learned

When North Carolina became a royal colony, its Assembly struggled with the new royal governor.

Now You Will Learn

During the mid-1700s, the colonies united under British rule to defeat French and Native American forces.

Preview Terms & Names

- **George Washington:** colonial military leader
- **French and Indian War:** England's war against the French and their Native American allies
- **Benjamin Franklin:** Pennsylvania delegate to the Albany Congress
- **Treaty of Paris:** ended the Seven Years' War

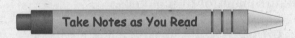

Take Notes as You Read

1.

Sequencing Events: The French and Indian War		
1754	**1760**	**1763**

The French and Indian War begins

In 1754, Governor Dinwiddie of Virginia demanded that the French leave the Ohio River valley. The French refused to leave.

Governor Dinwiddie ordered George Washington to build a fort on the Ohio River. Washington attacked France's nearby Fort Duquesne. Washington's men were defeated. This began the French and Indian War. The British fought against the French and their Native American allies.

In 1756, Britain and France officially declared war on each other. The conflict spread. It became the Seven Years' War, a global struggle for world power.

The Albany Congress

Before Washington attacked Fort Duquesne, colonial and Iroquois delegates met in Albany, New York, to discuss a defense against France. Benjamin Franklin presented the Albany Plan of Union. Franklin's plan called for a Grand Council of delegates headed by a president appointed by the king. Most colonial assemblies did not support Franklin's plan.

2. How did the French and Indian War begin?

_____

_____

CHAPTER 9

North Carolina responds to Virginia's call for help; Braddock's defeat

After Washington's defeat, Governor Dinwiddie asked other colonies for support. North Carolina sent 450 troops led by Colonel James Innes. Washington and Innes built Fort Cumberland on the Potomac River.

General Edward Braddock planned to join Washington and Innes and lead an attack against Fort Duquesne. However, many of Braddock's soldiers were killed by French and Native Americans on the way.

North Carolina suffers from Indian raids

After Braddock's defeat, Native Americans began attacking North Carolina settlers. Fort Dobbs was built as a refuge from raids. Fighting broke out between Virginians and the Cherokees who had joined them in a raid in Ohio. Then in 1760, full-scale war began between the Cherokee and the British. In 1761, a large British force defeated the Cherokee.

Britain triumphs; Peace treaties

In 1758, Major Hugh Waddell and 300 North Carolinians drove the French out of Fort Duquesne. The British renamed it Fort Pitt, and it eventually grew into the city of Pittsburgh. Britain also took control of most of New France, or Canada.

In 1763, Britain and France signed a treaty, which officially ended the Seven Years' War. Governor Dobbs of North Carolina signed a peace treaty with the Cherokee and the Catawba. Colonists were pleased, but this happiness would end when they learned of Britain's plans for the colonies.

3. **DRAW YOUR ANSWER** Draw a symbol that shows the purpose of the Treaty of Paris.

LOOK Closer

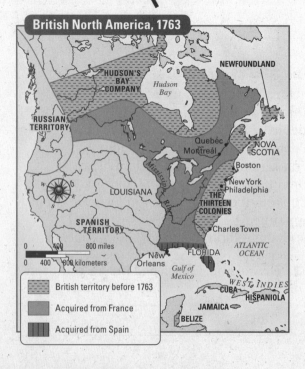

British North America, 1763

Mark It Up!

4. This map shows territories that Britain acquired on its own from France and from Spain.
   - **Circle** the lands that Britain acquired from France.
   - **Underline** the name of the territory that Britain acquired from Spain.
   - **Write** the names of the four cities located in the thirteen colonies.

_____

_____

Copyright © by McDougal Littell, a division of Houghton Mifflin Company

SECTION
3

The Road to Revolution
For use with pages 167–173

Before, You Learned

During the mid-1700s, the colonies united under British rule to defeat French and Native American forces.

Now You Will Learn

Seeking representative government and fair taxation, colonists banded together to protest British rule.

Preview Terms & Names

- **Sugar Act:** law that forced colonists to pay taxes on molasses and other goods
- **Quartering Act:** law that required colonists to shelter and feed British troops
- **Stamp Act:** law that stated colonists had to pay for stamps on taxable paper items
- **treason:** betrayal of one's country

Take Notes as You Read

1.

Sequencing Events: The Road to Revolution				
Stamp Act Congress	→	**1770**	→	**1773**

A new proclamation; Britain's new colonial policy

To avoid future wars with Native Americans, King George III signed the Proclamation of 1763. It declared land west of the Appalachian Mountains temporarily off-limits to settlers.

In 1764, Britain sent 10,000 troops to protect colonists and to enforce unpopular British laws. Britain also decided to raise taxes in the colonies to help pay its war debt.

The Sugar Act and the Quartering Act; The Stamp Act

- 1764: The Sugar Act raised duties on luxury items and gave inspectors the right to search colonial warehouses.

- 1765: The Quartering Act made colonists feed and shelter British troops.
- 1765: The Stamp Act went into effect even though colonists protested it.
- Colonists believed that only their own assemblies had the right to tax them.

2. In your own words, explain why colonists protested the new British taxes.

_____

_____

_____

The effect of the Stamp Act; Protest in North Carolina

Colonists attacked Britain's right to tax the colonies, risking being charged with treason, or betrayal of one's country. In 1765, Massachusetts invited delegates to a Stamp Act Congress to protest Parliament's right to tax the colonies. No delegate from North Carolina attended, but the colony still protested the Stamp Act. Parliament withdrew the act in 1766.

New taxes; North Carolina reaction; Non-Importation Association

In 1767, Britain passed the Townshend Acts. These acts raised taxes on goods to pay royal officials' salaries. Colonists protested with a boycott, or refusal to buy certain items. The North Carolina Assembly wrote to the king requesting "no taxation without representation." Assembly members approved a Non-Importation Association to boycott British goods.

The Boston Massacre; Tea parties

In 1770, Britain ended all taxes except the tea tax. Soon after, five colonists were killed in the Boston Massacre, a dispute with British soldiers.

In December 1773, colonists protested the tea tax by dumping tea into Boston Harbor. Some North Carolina women vowed to not drink tea. It was largely through women's efforts that the boycotts succeeded.

The "Intolerable Acts"; Conflict

The king sealed off Boston Harbor and placed Massachusetts under military control. Colonists responded by organizing the First Continental Congress. North Carolina agreed to attend. Soon, its last royal governor fled the colony. The colonists were creating their own American identity.

3. Explain the cause of colonial protests.

_____

_____

_____

LOOk Closer

PRIMARY SOURCE

> I see by the newspapers the Edenton ladies have signalized themselves by their protest against tea-drinking. . . . Is there a female Congress at Edenton too? I hope not for we Englishmen are afraid of the male Congress, but if the ladies . . . should attack us, the most fatal consequence is to be dreaded. . . . The only security on our side . . . is the probability that there are but few places in America which possess such female artillery as Edenton.
>
> Arthur Iredell, *"Letter to his brother"*

Mark It Up!

4. **Read** the primary source quotation.
   - **Circle** the source from which Iredell learned of the Edenton protest.
   - **Draw** a box around the person to whom Iredell wrote this letter.
   - **Underline** words and phrases that show that Iredell actually doubts the women's ability to bring about change.

SECTION 1

The Fighting Begins
For use with pages 179–185

Before, You Learned

Seeking representative government and fair taxation, colonists protested British rule.

Now You Will Learn

The colonies were soon fighting a revolution on the battlefield and through the Declaration of Independence.

Preview Terms & Names

- **minuteman:** a colonist trained to fight the British
- **Loyalist:** colonist who sided with Britain
- **Patriot:** colonist who wanted independence
- **Continental Congress:** representatives from the colonies who voted to declare independence
- **Declaration of Independence:** document that declared the colonies free and independent states

CHAPTER 10

Take Notes as You Read

1.

Identifying Problems and Solutions	
Problem: Colonists learned that British troops were coming to Lexington and Concord.	**Solution:**
Problem: After the Declaration of Independence, North Carolina had to create its own laws and government.	**Solution:**

The battles of Lexington and Concord

Few colonists wanted a war with Britain. Yet, ordinary citizens, called minutemen, armed themselves and trained to fight.

- April 18, 1775: British troops marched to Lexington, Massachusetts, to arrest leaders of the Sons of Liberty.
- The Sons of Liberty sent minutemen to meet the troops. A shot was fired, starting the Battle of Lexington.
- British troops marched to Concord to search for the colonists' weapons.
- Minutemen killed and wounded many British troops returning to Boston.
- These battles started a revolution.

The Second Continental Congress

At the Second Continental Congress, representatives hoped to deal with the growing threat of war. Fighting spread even as they planned. On June 14, 1775, the Congress voted to create the Continental Army, led by George Washington.

2. In your own words, explain why British troops came to Lexington and Concord.

_____

_____

The battles of Bunker Hill and Moores Creek Bridge

The Battle of Bunker Hill took place on June 17, 1775. The British attacked a fort that Americans had secretly built. The Americans fought bravely but ran out of gunpowder. Americans lost, but they proved that they could fight a trained army.

After Bunker Hill, the war spread. Loyalists, or people loyal to Britain, clashed with Patriots, who wanted independence. The first battle in North Carolina took place on February 27, 1776, at Moores Creek Bridge. Patriots defeated a group of Loyalists. This battle helped prevent the British from gaining control of the South.

British departure; The Halifax Resolves

Soon after Moores Creek Bridge, George Washington drove the British out of Boston. His troops surrounded Boston with 50 cannons. The British left for Canada on March 17, 1776. A few weeks later, a group of Patriots passed the Halifax Resolves, which recommended that all colonies declare independence from Britain.

The Declaration of Independence; The North Carolina Constitution of 1776

Thomas Jefferson wrote the Declaration of Independence. Approved by the Continental Congress on July 4, 1776, the document explained why colonists separated from Britain and listed the new states' rights.

Each of the thirteen new states had to create new governments. North Carolina's first constitution gave most of the power to the Assembly. All free men who paid taxes, including free African Americans, could vote for House members. The constitution was adopted on December 18, 1776.

3. **DRAW YOUR ANSWER** Draw a picture that shows how George Washington forced the British to leave Boston.

LOOk Closer

PRIMARY SOURCE

Gentlemen may cry, Peace, peace! but there is no peace. The war is actually begun! The next gale that sweeps from the north will bring to our ears the clash of resounding arms! Our brethren are already in the field! Why stand here idle? What is it that gentlemen wish? What would they have? Is life so dear or peace so sweet as to be purchased at the price of chains and slavery? Forbid it, Almighty God. I know not what course others may take, but as for me, give me liberty or give me death!

Patrick Henry, "Speech to the Virginia Convention"

Mark It Up!

4. **Read** the primary source quotation.
   - **Circle** the audience that heard this speech.
   - **Underline** two words that Henry uses to describe life under British rule.
   - **What** do you think Henry wants colonists to do?

   _____

   _____

SECTION 2 — The Fighting Spreads to North Carolina
For use with pages 190–195

Before, You Learned

After several battles, the colonies were soon fighting a revolution.

Now You Will Learn

The first battles of the Revolution were fought in the North, and then fighting spread to the Southern states.

Preview Terms & Names

- **George Rogers Clark:** led troops in the Appalachians
- **John Paul Jones:** first American naval hero
- **Lord Charles Cornwallis:** given the mission to attack North Carolina for the British
- **partisan:** Patriot followers
- **Nathanael Greene:** commander of the Continental Army in the South

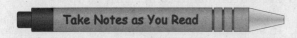

Take Notes as You Read

1.

Identifying Opportunities and Outcomes	
Opportunity: Three British armies planned to meet in Albany, then cut off the New England Colonies.	**Outcome:** On October 17, 1777,
Opportunity: British general Cornwallis	**Outcome:** Patriots defeated Cornwallis at the Battle of Kings Mountain.

War in the North

In the summer of 1776, British troops attacked New York. Defeated, Washington and his men escaped to Pennsylvania. Many Patriots feared they might lose the war.

On Christmas night 1776, Washington surprised a group of Hessians, German soldiers fighting for the British, in Trenton, New Jersey. Washington's men won the Battle of Trenton.

Britain planned to use three armies to cut off New England from the other colonies. However, Patriots forced one army to surrender at the Battle of Saratoga. This was a turning point in the war.

War in the West and at sea

George Rogers Clark and his men captured several British forts in the summer of 1778. His victories placed more land in the West under American control.

At sea, Americans used privateers, or trading ships, to hunt down British supply ships. John Paul Jones became the first American naval hero when his ship defeated a British warship in 1779.

2. Explain why the British failed to cut off New England from the rest of the colonies.

_____

_____

CHAPTER 10

War in the South

By the spring of 1779, the British had taken control of Georgia as well as Charles Town, South Carolina. Lord Charles Cornwallis was left in charge of Charles Town. His mission was to take control of North Carolina. He decided to wait for cooler weather before he attacked.

North Carolina prepares for invasion; Cornwallis invades North Carolina

While Cornwallis waited, North Carolina Patriots rallied their forces. Leaders gathered partisans, or Patriot followers, from neighboring counties. Fighting soon broke out between partisans and Loyalists. General Horatio Gates led his men into South Carolina, where they were defeated by British troops.

Cornwallis invaded North Carolina on September 8, 1780. Few Loyalists supported him. His men were defeated by Patriots at the Battle of Kings Mountain. They retreated.

The Battle of Guilford Courthouse

After Kings Mountain, Washington made Nathanael Greene commander of the Continental Army in the South. On March 15, 1781, his troops fought Cornwallis at the Battle of Guilford Courthouse. Cornwallis won, but both sides retreated. Greene led his men back into South Carolina. This left most of Georgia and the Carolinas in American hands.

3. In your own words, explain why Cornwallis retreated from North Carolina in 1780.

   _____

   _____

   _____

LOOk Cl⊕ser

PRIMARY SOURCE

These are the times that try men's souls. The summer soldier and the sunshine patriot will, in this crisis, shrink from the service of their country; but he that stands it now, deserves the love and thanks of man and woman.

Thomas Paine, *"The American Crisis"*

✎ Mark It Up!

4. In this quotation, Paine describes two different types of people.
   - **Read** the primary source quotation.
   - **Circle** the two names Paine gives to soldiers who give up defending their country.
   - **Underline** the reward Paine believes brave soldiers will receive.

CHAPTER 10

SECTION 3

The Colonists' Victory and Its Impact

For use with pages 198–203

Before, You Learned

The first battles were fought in the North, and then fighting spread to Southern states.

Now You Will Learn

Americans won the war, creating the need for a strong national government.

Preview Terms & Names

- **Yorktown:** port between the York and James rivers on a narrow peninsula in Chesapeake Bay where Cornwallis surrendered to Americans
- **blockade:** the blocking of an entrance to prevent supplies or people from reaching a site
- **Treaty of Paris:** 1783 treaty that ended the Revolutionary War

Take Notes as You Read

1.

Identifying Problems and Solutions

Problem: Cornwallis waited in Yorktown to receive supplies from Britain.	→	Solution:
Problem:	→	Solution: Britain and America signed the Treaty of Paris in 1783.

Before and after the Battle of Yorktown

Cornwallis led his army to Yorktown to wait for fresh supplies from Britain. At the same time, a large French army joined American troops and marched to Virginia. French warships formed a blockade in Chesapeake Bay. Cornwallis was trapped; no British ships could reach him. The French and American troops attacked. On October 19, 1781, thousands of British soldiers surrendered. The Patriots had won the American Revolution.

Fighting did not end in the South after the Battle of Yorktown. In North Carolina, Loyalists and Patriots continued to fight. In 1782, the British gave up Charles Town and Savannah.

The Treaty of Paris

The Treaty of Paris was signed on September 3, 1783, by Britain and the United States. Britain recognized the independence of the thirteen colonies. The Americans agreed that Loyalists would not be punished after the war. Britain and America also agreed to pay back any money they owed each other. The last British troops left in November 1783.

2. DRAW YOUR ANSWER Draw a picture that shows the purpose of the Treaty of Paris.

Reasons for America's victory

Americans won the Revolutionary War for several reasons:

- They had courage and persistence.
- They had the advantage of fighting on familiar territory.
- The British had to send supplies and military orders back and forth across the Atlantic Ocean, which took months.
- Fewer British people supported the war as it became more expensive.
- Americans had learned new fighting tactics during a previous war.
- Washington was a more effective leader than Cornwallis.

Help from abroad, and will to win

France helped America win the war by sending troops, money, and help from its navy. After France, Spain and the Netherlands also joined the war against Britain.

The Americans had more reason to fight than the British. The colonists were fighting to protect their families and homes. They were fighting for themselves and for the future.

Impact of the Revolution

The American Revolution affected future expansion of the United States. It also created a very large debt. Tens of thousands of colonists were killed or wounded.

The war also caused people to think about other issues, such as religious freedom and slavery. Some states freed slaves while others defended slavery.

The biggest concern was how to create a strong national government. This new government would have to guarantee people's right to rule themselves and protect their freedoms.

3. In your own words, explain two advantages that Americans had during the war.

_____

_____

_____

L⊙⊙k Cl⊕ser

Surrounding of Yorktown

- Lafayette
- Williamsburg
- Gloucester
- Yorktown
- Washington and de Rochambeau
- *Jamestown Island*
- *James River*
- Hampton
- Cape Charles
- Chesapeake Bay
- ATLANTIC OCEAN
- Cape Henry
- Norfolk
- Portsmouth
- De Grasse
- 76°W
- 37°N
- 0   5   10 miles
- 0   5   10 kilometers

Legend:
- British forces under Cornwallis
- American and French forces
- American and French troop movements
- British fleet
- French fleet

✎ Mark It Up!

4. This map shows British, American, and French troops on land and at sea at the Battle of Yorktown.
   - **Circle** Cornwallis's troops.
   - **Draw** a box around the French ships that formed a blockade.
   - On which river did Washington travel to reach Yorktown?

_____

SECTION 1

Writing a Constitution
For use with pages 209–213

Before, You Learned
Americans won their independence, creating the need for a national government.

Now You Will Learn
Delegates to the Constitutional Convention strengthened the federal government.

Preview Terms & Names

- **constitution:** a written plan of government
- **Articles of Confederation:** created the national government
- **Congress:** established by the Articles of Confederation
- **Great Compromise:** divided Congress into the Senate and House of Representatives

Take Notes as You Read

1.

Identifying Problems and Solutions		
Problem: The national government created by the Articles of Confederation was not strong enough.	→	**Solution:**
Problem:	→	**Solution:** The delegates agreed to the Great Compromise, which created two houses in Congress.

Articles of Confederation are drawn up; Troubles spark rebellion

In 1777, the Second Continental Congress created the Articles of Confederation. The articles divided power between the national government and the state governments. The states had most of the power. Congress, the one body of national government established by the articles, had little power. Congress did not have the right to collect taxes and control trade.

Without tax money, Congress could not pay for the American Revolution. Without the power to regulate trade, it could not settle trade disputes. People worried about foreign invasion or states declaring themselves independent countries. George Washington

argued that a national government could bring the union together.

In Massachusetts, landowners had to pay high taxes. Some even had to sell their land in order to pay the taxes. In January 1787, a group of angry farmers led by Daniel Shays tried to seize guns. The state asked Congress to get involved, but Congress did not have the power to help.

2. Explain two important powers given to the states under the Articles of Confederation.

_____

_____

CHAPTER 11

The Constitutional Convention is held

The Constitutional Convention met in 1787 to decide how to give the national government more power. The delegates concluded that the government should have three parts: a congress, a president, and a court system. No one person or group could become too powerful.

3. In your own words, explain why the delegates divided the government into three parts.

_____

_____

The Great Compromise

The Great Compromise created a two-house Congress. In the Senate, each state would have two members. In the House of Representatives, the number of members from each state would be based on population.

Slavery in the Constitution

The Three-Fifths Compromise meant that three-fifths of the total number of slaves would determine taxes and representation in the House. The delegates decided that Congress could not ban slavery until 1808.

The role of the president

- Electors would vote for the president.
- The president could veto bills, but Congress could override a veto with a two-thirds majority vote.
- The president could be removed from office if necessary.

The Constitution still had to be approved by nine states before it could become law.

4. **DRAW YOUR ANSWER** Draw a picture that shows one way the Constitution limited the president's power.

LOOk Cl⊕ser

✎Mark It Up!

5. This illustration shows the takeover of a Massachusetts courthouse by the followers of Daniel Shays.
   - **Reread** the section titled "Money troubles spark rebellion."
   - **Write** a caption below the painting that explains the reason for the rebellion.

CHAPTER 11

Name _____ Date _____

Ratifying the Constitution
For use with pages 214–218

Before, You Learned
Delegates to the Constitutional Convention strengthened the federal government.

Now You Will Learn
The Constitution set up the federal system of government. Amendments protect people's rights.

Preview Terms & Names

- **Federalist:** person who supported the new Constitution
- **Antifederalist:** person who opposed the Constitution
- **Bill of Rights:** the first ten Constitutional amendments
- **checks and balances:** the balancing of power and the checking of one branch by another

Take Notes as You Read

1.

Identifying Situations and Outcomes

Situation: North Carolina and Rhode Island did not approve the Constitution in 1787.	→	Outcome:
Situation: Individual Rights:	→	Outcome: Amendments to the Constitution:

The debate continues

At the state conventions in 1787, representatives debated the new plan of government. Federalists supported the new Constitution, believing it balanced power between the national and state governments.

Antifederalists disagreed with the supporters of the Constitution. They argued that the Constitution gave too much power to a central government. Without a bill of rights, Antifederalists argued, the Constitution did not protect the liberty of individual citizens.

The Constitution is approved

By the end of July 1788, every state except North Carolina and Rhode Island had approved the Constitution. When Congress agreed to consider adding a bill of rights, North Carolina approved the Constitution. This took place on November 21, 1789. Rhode Island did not approve the Constitution until May 1790.

2. In your own words, explain why Antifederalists believed a bill of rights should be added to the Constitution.

_____

_____

CHAPTER 11

CHAPTER 11 SECTION 2: RATIFYING THE CONSTITUTION, *CONTINUED*

The first president takes office

The states held elections for senators, representatives, and electors. The electors voted for George Washington to become the first president of the United States. He was sworn into office on April 30, 1789 in New York City, the nation's first capital.

The Bill of Rights is added

In 1791, Congress added ten amendments, or changes, to the Constitution. These are known as the Bill of Rights. They guarantee rights such as freedom of speech, freedom of religion, and freedom of press. With the Bill of Rights, the people had truly won the rights that they had fought for during the American Revolution.

3. **DRAW YOUR ANSWER** Draw a picture that represents one freedom protected in the Bill of Rights.

The new government begins its work

The Constitution set up a federal system that divided power between the national and state governments. The national government was made up of three branches. The legislative branch is Congress. It makes laws and treaties, coins money, and controls trade. The executive branch includes the president and vice-president. They make sure that the laws are obeyed. The judicial branch is the national system of courts and makes sure laws obey the Constitution.

Dividing the power prevents one branch from becoming too powerful. It also allows each branch to check on the others. This is called a system of checks and balances.

4. In your own words, explain the purpose of the judicial branch of the government.

_____

_____

LOOk Closer

We the People of the United States, in order to form a more perfect Union, establish justice, insure domestic tranquility, provide for the common defense, promote the general welfare, and secure the blessings of liberty to ourselves and our posterity, do ordain and establish this Constitution for the United States of America.

Preamble to the Constitution

Mark It Up!

5. Read the primary source quotation.
   - **Circle** the group named in this sentence.
   - **Place check marks** beside the six goals of the Constitution.
   - **Underline** the part of the preamble that tells what the group is doing to make sure the goals are met.

Copyright © by McDougal Littell, a division of Houghton Mifflin Company

CHAPTER 11

SECTION 3

Heading West: The Louisiana Purchase

For use with pages 219–222

Before, You Learned

The Constitution set up the federal system of government. Amendments protect people's rights.

Now You Will Learn

After the Louisiana Purchase, people explored land west of the Mississippi River.

Preview Terms & Names

- **Thomas Jefferson:** President responsible for the Louisiana Purchase
- **Louisiana Purchase:** land purchase that doubled the size of the United States
- **Meriwether Lewis and William Clark:** led an expedition of the Missouri River in hopes of finding a water route across the continent

Take Notes as You Read

1.

Identifying Situations and Outcomes	
Situation: President Jefferson asked the French to sell New Orleans to the United States.	**Outcome:**
Situation: the new territory:	**Outcome:** groups of explorers:

The importance of the Mississippi River; The Louisiana Purchase

The Mississippi River became important as more Americans settled west of the Appalachians. People used the river to ship goods to New Orleans, where the goods could then be shipped to the east coast and overseas.

Before returning New Orleans to the French, Spain closed the city to American shipping. Many called for war against France and Spain.

President Thomas Jefferson offered to buy New Orleans from France. Napoleon Bonaparte, France's ruler, agreed to sell

the city along with all of the Louisiana Territory. Jefferson was thrilled. He knew the country needed land for its many farmers. However, he worried that the Constitution did not give the president the power to buy land. On April 30, 1803, the Louisiana Purchase was approved. It doubled the size of the United States.

2. In your own words, explain one reason why Thomas Jefferson made the Louisiana Purchase.

_____

_____

_____

CHAPTER 11

The Lewis and Clark expedition

Jefferson sent an expedition, led by Captain Meriwether Lewis and Lieutenant William Clark, to explore the new territory with the goal of finding a water route across the continent. The explorers crossed the northern part of the territory, across the Rocky Mountains and reached the Columbia River.

The Pike expedition

Zebulon Pike led an expedition to explore the southern part of the Louisiana Territory. He and his men were arrested after crossing into Spanish territory as they tried to reach the Red River. Pike brought back descriptions of the Great Plains and the Rio Grande Valley.

3. Explain one difference between the Lewis and Clark and the Pike expeditions.

   _____

   _____

The effects of exploration

Exploration led to:
- good maps of the Louisiana Territory
- increased interest in the fur trade
- Pike's incorrect labeling of the Great Plains as a desert led many to believe the Plains were useless for farming.

The impact on North Carolina

As new territories grew large enough to apply for statehood, they had to choose whether to allow slavery. Many people feared that Congress could move to ban slavery throughout the nation.

4. **DRAW YOUR ANSWER** Draw a picture that represents one of the effects of exploration in the Louisiana Territory.

LOOk Cl⊕ser

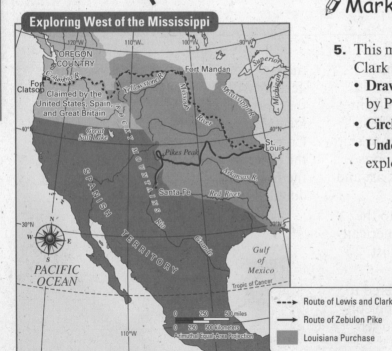

Exploring West of the Mississippi

✎ Mark It Up!

5. This map shows the routes of the Lewis and Clark and the Pike expeditions.
   - **Draw** arrows next to the route traveled by Pike.
   - **Circle** the route taken by Lewis and Clark.
   - **Underline** the names of two rivers explored by Lewis and Clark.

SECTION
4
The War of 1812
For use with pages 223–227

Before, You Learned
After the Louisiana Purchase, people began to explore west of the Mississippi River.

Now You Will Learn
Tension between America and Britain increased, and the nations went to war in 1812.

Preview Terms & Names

- **Embargo Act of 1807:** law that stopped all American foreign trade
- **Tecumseh:** Shawnee chief who united Native American tribes to fight white settlers
- **War Hawks:** Westerners who demanded war against Britain
- **Andrew Jackson:** led an army against the British
- **Battle of New Orleans:** last battle of the War of 1812

Take Notes as You Read

1.

Identifying Problems and Solutions	
Problem: While they were at war, Britain and France both used blockades on America.	**Solution:** 1807:
Problem: British offenses:	**Solution:** War of 1812:

Tensions between Britain and the United States continue

After the American Revolution, neither America nor Britain followed the peace treaty. The British kept forts west of the Appalachian Mountains, where they traded with Native Americans. Americans feared and resented this trade.

War between Britain and France affects the United States

France and Britain were at war between 1793 and 1814. Both sides formed blockades to prevent America from sending supplies to its enemy. Britain also used impressment, or kidnapping, to force American sailors to work on British ships. Many Americans demanded war against Britain.

Trade as a weapon

Instead of declaring war against Britain, Jefferson used the Embargo Act of 1807 to stop all foreign trade. However, this hurt Americans more than it hurt the British or the French. Congress repealed the law, but American anger toward Britain continued.

2. In your own words, explain why the Embargo Act of 1807 was unsuccessful.

_____

_____

CHAPTER 11

Tecumseh and Native American unity

A Shawnee chief named Tecumseh organized Native American tribes to fight white settlers in Ohio and Indiana. Many Americans believed the British encouraged this resistance. After the Shawnee were defeated at the Battle of Tippecanoe, they fled to Canada. There, the British welcomed them.

War Hawks; War with Britain begins

Westerners, known as War Hawks, demanded war against Britain. They wanted to stop British aid to Native Americans. Others demanded war because of British violations of American rights at sea.

Congress declared war on Britain on June 18, 1812. In August 1814, the British captured and burned the White House and the Capitol in Washington, D.C. Americans defeated British troops in battles at Fort McHenry and Lake Champlain.

The Battle of New Orleans

In December 1814, British ships attacked the port of New Orleans. General Andrew Jackson led an army against them. Jackson's men won the Battle of New Orleans on January 8, 1815. However, the battle had been unnecessary. The Treaty of Ghent had ended the war two weeks before, but the news had been delayed by slow mail from Europe.

Consequences of the war

- No territory changed hands, and there was no clear winner.
- The British stopped impressments.
- The war contributed to regional differences between New England, the South, and the West.
- American manufacturing grew as people made more of their own goods.

4. DRAW YOUR ANSWER Draw a picture of one outcome of the War of 1812.

LO☉k Cl⊕ser

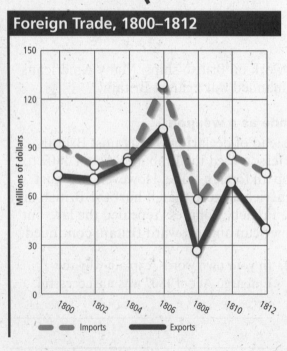

Foreign Trade, 1800–1812

Millions of dollars — (y-axis: 0, 30, 60, 90, 120, 150)
(x-axis: 1800, 1802, 1804, 1806, 1808, 1810, 1812)

- - - Imports   ⬛ Exports

✐ Mark It Up!

5. This graph shows the value of American imports and exports between 1800 and 1812.
   - **Circle** the year when the amount of imports and exports sold was the **least**.
   - **Underline** the type of trade that had the **most** value in 1812.
   - **Write** the difference between imports and exports in 1806.

   _____

CHAPTER 11

SECTION
1

Seven Principles of the Constitution
For use with pages 234–237

Before, You Learned

Leaders known as the Framers wrote the U.S. Constitution.

Now You Will Learn

The Framers of the Constitution used seven principles to guide them as they created a new system of government.

- **popular sovereignty:** government ruled by the people
- **federalism:** system in which power is divided between a central government and other political units
- **separation of powers:** division of basic government roles into branches
- **checks and balances:** system in which each branch of government can exercise control over the others

Take Notes as You Read

1.

FINDING MAIN IDEAS	
Topic	**Main Idea**
Government power	
Rights of the people	The Constitution protects people's individual rights and freedoms in the Bill of Rights.

Popular Sovereignty

The Framers based the Constitution on the principle of popular sovereignty—a government in which the people rule. As the nation changed and grew, a broader range of Americans shared in the power to govern themselves.

Republicanism

The Framers wanted to give the people a voice in government and preserve sound decision making. They looked to republicanism to give people power to vote for representatives who work in the government.

Federalism

Federalism divided power between the federal government and the states.

- The Constitution gives delegated powers to the national government.
- Powers kept by the states are called reserved powers.
- Powers shared by both are known as concurrent powers.

2. Why did the Framers include the principle of federalism in the Constitution?

_____

_____

CHAPTER CH

Separation of Powers

The Framers did not want one group to have too much power; they used separation of powers. The Constitution divides the government into three branches. Articles 1, 2, and 3 explain how powers are split.

Checks and Balances

The Framers included a system of checks and balances in the Constitution to make sure that the branches work together fairly. Each branch can check, or use control over, the other branches. For example, only Congress can pass laws. Yet the president can check this power by refusing to sign it.

3. **DRAW YOUR ANSWER** Draw a symbol that represents checks and balances.

Limited Government

The Framers also used the idea of limited government. According to this principle, everyone—ordinary citizens and powerful leaders alike—must obey the law. People or groups cannot change or avoid the law to serve their own interests.

Individual Rights

The first ten amendments to the Constitution protect people from a government that is too powerful. Called the Bill of Rights, they guarantee certain individual rights, or personal liberties and privileges. For example, government cannot control what people say or write.

4. In your own words, explain two ways the Constitution limits the government's power.

_____

_____

L☉☉k Cl⊕ser

Separation of Powers

United States Constitution

Article 1
LEGISLATIVE BRANCH
Congress makes laws.

Article 2
EXECUTIVE BRANCH
President enforces the law.

Article 3
JUDICIAL BRANCH
Supreme Court interprets the law.

✐ Mark It Up!

5. This diagram shows how the Constitution divides power among the three branches of the government.
   • **Circle** the branch that creates laws.

   • **Underline** the powers of the judicial branch.
   • Which article explains the powers given to the president?

_____

CHAPTER CH

SECTION 2

The Constitution of the United States
For use with pages 238–257

Before, You Learned
The Framers of the Constitution used seven principles to guide them as they created a new government.

Now You Will Learn
The Constitution as written by the Framers includes a preamble and seven articles.

Preview Terms & Names

- **preamble:** introduction
- **article:** a part of a document
- **inferior courts:** courts with less power than the Supreme Court
- **ratification:** approval

Take Notes as You Read

1.

FINDING MAIN IDEAS	
Article	**Main Idea**
Article 4	
Article 7	Nine states must approve the Constitution before it can become law.

Preamble
The Preamble explains that the people of the United States establish the Constitution. The Preamble also lists goals for the nation, which include making fair laws and protecting the country.

Article 1: The Legislature
Article 1 of the Constitution explains the powers of the legislature, the branch of government that makes laws. Legislative power is given to Congress, which is divided into the Senate and the House of Representatives. Article 1 also lists the powers given to Congress and describes how bills become laws.

Article 2: The Executive
Article 2 explains the powers of the executive branch. It also describes how the president is chosen, lists the president's duties and powers, and explains the impeachment process.

Article 3: The Judiciary
Article 3 describes the powers of the judiciary, the branch of government that interprets the law. The judiciary is made up of the Supreme Court and inferior courts.

2. Explain the purpose of Articles 1, 2, and 3.

_____

_____

CHAPTER CH

Article 4: Relations Among States

Article 4 describes how the states will work together. This article explains that states will respect the laws of other states. Article 4 also describes the process of admitting new states and guarantees each state a republican form of government.

Article 5: Amending the Constitution

Article 5 explains the process of amending, or making changes to, the Constitution. Amendments can be proposed, or suggested, by a two-thirds vote in either Congress or the state legislatures. Amendments must be ratified, or approved, by three-fourths of the states.

3. **DRAW YOUR ANSWER** Draw a diagram that shows how an amendment is ratified.

Article 6: Supremacy of the National Government

Article 6 explains the supremacy, or highest authority, of the national government. It states that the Constitution has power over all state constitutions, laws, and courts.

Article 7: Ratification

Article 7 explains that nine states had to ratify, or approve, the Constitution. This article is followed by the signatures of 39 men, including President George Washington and representatives from the states.

4. In your own words, explain how Article 6 limits the powers of the states.

_____

_____

LOOk Closer

Comparing Federal and State Powers
Americans live under both national and state governments.

NATIONAL POWERS
- Maintain military
- Declare war
- Establish postal system
- Set standards for weights and measures
- Protect copyrights and patents

SHARED POWERS
- Collect taxes
- Establish courts
- Regulate interstate commerce
- Regulate banks
- Borrow money
- Provide for the general welfare
- Punish criminals

STATE POWERS
- Establish local governments
- Set up schools
- Regulate state commerce
- Make regulations for marriage
- Establish and regulate corporations

Mark It Up!

5. This diagram compares and contrasts the powers given to the national and state governments.
   - **Circle** the powers given to the states.

- **Underline** three powers shared by both national and state governments.
- Which part of the government has authority over the U.S. postal system?

_____

SECTION
3
The Bill of Rights and Amendments 11–27
For use with pages 258–269

Before, You Learned
The Constitution as written by the Framers includes a preamble and seven articles.

Now You Will Learn
The articles of the Constitution are followed by 27 amendments, or additions.

Preview Terms & Names

- **naturalized:** made a citizen of a country
- **abolish:** to end completely
- **repeal:** to reverse

 Take Notes as You Read

1.

FINDING MAIN IDEAS	
Amendments	**Main Idea**
The Bill of Rights	The people of the United States are guaranteed certain personal liberties and rights.
Amendment 15 and Amendment 19	

The Bill of Rights
The first ten amendments to the Constitution are known as the Bill of Rights. These amendments, added in 1791, protect the individual freedoms of all citizens.

Amendment
1: Religious and Political Freedom
2: Right to Bear Arms
3: Quartering Troops
4: Search and Seizure
5: Rights of Accused Persons
6: Right to a Speedy, Public Trial
7: Trial by Jury in Civil Cases
8: Limits of Fines and Punishments

9: Rights of People
10: Powers of States and People

Amendments 11, 12, and 13
Amendment 11 (1795) gives federal courts the power to hear lawsuits against states. Amendment 12 (1804) explains that the electors cast separate votes for the president and the vice president. Amendment 13 (1865) abolishes slavery.

2. In your own words, explain one similarity between Amendment 6 and Amendment 7.

_____

_____

Copyright © by McDougal Littell, a division of Houghton Mifflin Company

CHAPTER CH

Amendments 14–20

- Amendment 14 (1868) protects the civil rights of citizens, people born or naturalized in the United States.
- Amendment 15 (1870) states that the right to vote cannot be denied based on race, color, or to the formerly enslaved.
- Amendment 16 (1913) gives Congress the power to tax people's income.
- Amendment 17 (1913) states that senators will be elected by the people.
- Amendment 18 (1919) prohibits the manufacture and sale of alcohol.
- Amendment 19 (1920) grants women the right to vote.
- Amendment 20 (1933) reduces the amount of time between a president or congressperson's election and the beginning of his or her term.

Amendments 21–27

- Amendment 21 (1933) repeals, or reverses, Amendment 18.
- Amendment 22 (1951) states that one president may only serve two terms.
- Amendment 23 (1961) allows the District of Columbia to choose electors.
- Amendment 24 (1964) abolishes poll taxes, or voting fees.
- Amendment 25 (1967) explains who will take over for the president if necessary.
- Amendment 26 (1971) lowers the voting age to 18.
- Amendment 27 (1992) prevents members of Congress from raising their own salaries.

3. Which amendment to the Constitution has been repealed?

_____

_____

LOOk Closer

Reconstruction Amendments

13th Amendment 1865
- Ended slavery in the United States

14th Amendment 1868
- Defined national and state citizenship
- Protected citizens' rights
- Promised equal protection of the laws

15th Amendment 1870
- Designed to protect African Americans' voting rights

✎ Mark It Up!

4. This diagram compares amendments that were passed during Reconstruction.
   - **Circle** the amendment that guarantees civil rights to all citizens.

   - **Underline** the purpose of the amendment passed in 1870.
   - When was slavery in the United States abolished?

_____

CHAPTER CH

SECTION
4

Citizenship Handbook
For use with pages 272–278

Before, You Learned
The articles of the Constitution are followed by 27 amendments, or changes.

Now You Will Learn
Certain responsibilities come along with the rights guaranteed to citizens by the Constitution.

Preview Terms & Names

- **responsibilities:** duties of all citizens
- **reason:** considering different points of view, using logic, and using good judgment
- **respect:** concern for one's self, for other people, and for the community

Take Notes as You Read

1.

FINDING MAIN IDEAS

Topic	Main Idea
Your rights	
Your responsibilities	

The Role of the Citizen
Citizens of the United States enjoy many basic rights and freedoms. They are expected to obey laws, vote, and serve on juries.

Reason and respect are also important. Reason includes thoughtfulness, logic, and good judgment. Respect for yourself, others, and your community affects how you participate in society.

Active Citizenship
People of all ages can be active citizens. You can follow five steps to be a model citizen.

1. Know your rights.
2. Be responsible.
3. Stay informed.
4. Make good decisions.
5. Take action in your community.

What Is a Citizen?
A citizen is a legal member of a nation who is loyal to that nation. A citizen is guaranteed certain rights. A child born in the United States is a citizen. A person born outside the United States can be naturalized, or made a citizen.

2. In your own words, explain two steps you can take to be a model citizen.

_____

_____

CHAPTER CH

What Are Your Rights and Responsibilities?

All citizens have three kinds of rights. These include civil rights, or basic freedoms, protection from unfair government actions, and equal treatment under the law. These rights have sensible limits.

All citizens must also carry out both personal and civic responsibilities. Civic responsibilities include obeying laws and paying taxes. Personal responsibilities include taking care of yourself and behaving in a respectful way.

3. DRAW YOUR ANSWER Draw a picture that shows one example of a civic responsibility.

Building Citizenship Skills

Good citizens stay informed, make good decisions, and take action in their communities.

- Stay informed: read, watch, or listen to accurate sources of information.
- Make good decisions: Do not make civic decisions on impulse. Follow a problem-solving process.
- Take action by following these steps:
1. Find a cause that interests you.
2. Develop a plan for solving the problem.
3. Follow through on your plans.

4. In your own words, explain how you can make good decisions.

_____

_____

_____

LOOk Closer

Responsibilities of a U.S. Citizen

UNDER 18
- Receive an education, either at school or at home.
- Take responsibility for one's behavior.
- Help one's family.

ALL AGES
- Obey rules and laws.
- Be tolerant of others.
- Pay taxes.
- Volunteer for a cause.
- Stay informed about issues.

OVER 18
- Vote.
- Serve on a jury.
- Serve in the military to defend the country.

✎ Mark It Up!

5. This diagram compares the responsibilities of citizens under 18 to those of citizens over 18.
  - **Circle** the responsibilities shared by all citizens of all ages.

- **Underline** two responsibilities of citizens under 18.
- At what age can a citizen be called to serve on a jury?

_____

SECTION 1

The Sleep of Indifference

For use with pages 285–289

Before, You Learned

Tension between America and Britain increased, and the two nations went to war in 1812.

Now You Will Learn

In the early 1800s, isolation, an agricultural economy, and slavery kept North Carolina from making advancements.

Preview Terms & Names

- **individualism:** concern with one's own needs and freedoms
- **legislature:** lawmaking branch of government
- **academy:** school paid for by individuals
- **economy:** the way people produce goods and services
- **Trail of Tears:** 1,200 mile journey taken by Cherokee forced to leave their homes

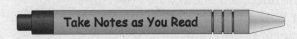
Take Notes as You Read

1.

FINDING MAIN IDEAS	
Event/Idea	**Details**
Cotton gin	faster way to clean cotton increased production; most farmers in North Carolina began to grow cotton; industry did not grow
Farming	
Cherokee relocation	

The impact of isolation; The attitude toward education

By 1832, North Carolina was behind other states in the area of education. Many could not read or write. People lived far apart, with few towns and little trade. This contributed to feelings of individualism, or concern with one's own needs and freedoms.

Many parents in North Carolina were uneducated. They preferred to have their children work on the farm instead of go to school. Landowners did not want to pay taxes to educate the children of poorer families. The legislature did not demand the creation of public schools. Instead, North Carolina had private schools called academies.

The state's economy

North Carolina's economy became more agricultural after the invention of the cotton gin. The cotton gin was a machine that removed the seeds from cotton much faster than workers could do by hand.

Most North Carolinians began growing cotton, and people lost interest in manufacturing. With the economy focused on cotton, industry did not grow.

2. Why did many parents in North Carolina think education was unimportant?

_____

_____

CHAPTER 12

Slavery's hidden costs; Farm conditions

Slavery also hurt North Carolina's economy. Wealthy landowners invested their money in this cruel and unjust system instead of developing industry or improving agriculture.

Farmers rarely made any attempt to improve their land or ensure that the soil would stay fertile. Poor roads and rivers discouraged farmers from bringing their goods to market. Most farmers only grew enough food for themselves.

3. In your own words, explain how slavery hurt North Carolina's economy.

_____

_____

The Cherokee are ordered to leave North Carolina; The Trail of Tears

In the early 1800s, most of the Cherokee in North Carolina lived in extremely poor conditions. In 1819, many Cherokee were forced to give up their claims to land. Then in 1830, President Jackson signed a law that required all Native Americans to move west of the Mississippi. The Cherokee won a challenge to the law, but the ruling was ignored, and in 1838, soldiers forced the Cherokee on a 1,200 mile march to their new home. More than 4,000 died on the journey known as the Trail of Tears.

A government undemocratic in form and spirit

North Carolina's political problems continued. The new state government did not fairly represent all the people. Wealthy easterners dominated the legislature. They looked down on the "common people." As the number of "common people" grew, they would demand a voice in government.

4. **DRAW YOUR ANSWER** Draw a symbol showing the effect of the Trail of Tears.

LOOk Closer

Mark It Up!

5. This illustration shows the Cherokee making the forced march to land west of the Mississippi River.
   - **Circle** examples of the three ways the Cherokee traveled on the march.
   - **Draw** arrows to three types of animals the Cherokee brought with them.
   - **Write** the letter *S* on one soldier in the painting.

SECTION 2   Archibald Murphey and the Beginnings of Reform

For use with pages 290–292

CHAPTER 12

Before, You Learned

In the early 1800s, North Carolina made few advancements.

Now You Will Learn

Archibald Murphey tried to reform North Carolina.

Preview Terms & Names

- **Archibald DeBow Murphey:** the leader of reform in North Carolina from 1815 to 1840
- **literary fund:** a fund used to establish the North Carolina public school system
- **internal improvement:** improvements to the state's infrastructure

Take Notes as You Read

1.

FINDING IMPORTANT DETAILS	
Topic	**Details**
Literary fund	Murphey fought for a public school system; Assembly started a literary fund in 1825; fund did not receive enough money
Transportation improvements	
Constitutional reform	

Preparation for leadership

From 1815 to 1840, a small group of reformers led by Archibald DeBow Murphey tried to solve North Carolina's problems. Murphey fought for a system of public education, internal improvements, and constitutional reform.

Murphey was raised and educated in North Carolina. He worked as a lawyer, a judge, and served in the General Assembly. Murphey was disturbed by the large numbers of poor, uneducated people in North Carolina. He became determined to fight for reform so that the state could improve.

The state's literary fund

Murphey believed in state-supported public education. He shared his ideas in a pamphlet called "Report on Education." In 1825, the General Assembly decided to set aside state money for a literary fund. It would be used for a public school system.

Unfortunately, the fund grew very slowly. Legislators did not pass bills to put more money into the fund. The fund was never able to pay for public schools throughout the state.

2. Explain why the literary fund failed.

_____

_____

_____

CHAPTER 12

Suggestions for internal improvements

In 1815, Murphey created a plan in which the state would pay to improve harbors and build canals and turnpikes. He also wanted to drain swamplands so they could be used for farming.

In 1819, the legislature started a fund for projects like these. Soon nearly every community in the state had a project to be funded. Unfortunately, the state chose the wrong projects to fund, and the program failed.

In the late 1820s and early 1830s, the locomotive engine was introduced to North Carolina. In 1834, the legislature chartered the first railroad company in the state.

3. **DRAW YOUR ANSWER** Draw a picture that shows one of the improvements suggested by Murphey.

The need for constitutional reform

The west wanted public schools and transportation. The east, which controlled the state, did not. Reform could not happen until the undemocratic constitution of North Carolina was changed. Murphey argued for a convention to discuss changing the constitution. His proposal was rejected.

Murphey's legacy

Murphey spent his life trying to find ways to improve life for all North Carolinians. He was unsuccessful because other people in power did not support his ideas. A political party soon emerged that brought about the progress that Murphey desired.

4. Explain why Murphey wanted to change North Carolina's constitution.

_____

_____

_____

LOOk Closer

PRIMARY SOURCE

> I know ten times as much of the Topography of this Circuit, as the Men who have lived here fifty years. I had no idea that we had such a poor, ignorant, squalid Population, as I have seen. . . . In the Towns are found decent and well informed Men in Matters of Business, Men who look well and live well. But the Mass of the Common People in the Country are lazy, sickly, poor, dirty, and ignorant. Yet this is a Section of the State upon which the Hand of Industry would soon impress a fine Character.
>
> Archibald D. Murphey,
> *"Letter to Thomas Ruffin"*

✏ Mark It Up!

5. Read the primary source quotation.
   - **Circle** two words or phrases Murphey uses to describe people in the towns.
   - **Underline** five words Murphey uses to describe people in the country.
   - **Draw** an arrow to the name of the person to whom this letter is written.

SECTION 3

The Constitution of 1835 and Its Impact
For use with pages 293–295

Before, You Learned
From 1815 to 1840, Archibald Murphey tried to reform North Carolina.

Now You Will Learn
The creation of a second political party and a new state constitution ended North Carolina's period of slow progress.

Preview Terms & Names

- **Whig Party:** political party whose members favored banks and internal improvements
- **David L. Swain:** became governor of North Carolina in 1832, supported constitutional reform
- **Nathaniel Macon:** president of the state constitutional convention of 1835

Take Notes as You Read

1.

SUPPORTING TOPICS WITH DETAILS	
Topic	**Details**
Whig Party	formed by people unhappy with President Jackson; members favored banks and improvements; strong western support
Demands of the west	
Convention of 1835	

Rise of a two-party system
For 20 years after the War of 1812, the Republican Party was the only political party in North Carolina. This started to change after Andrew Jackson was elected as the nation's president.

Many North Carolinians, especially those in the west, were disappointed by Jackson's leadership. Jackson opposed improvements like those that Archibald Murphey had supported.

Rise of the Whig Party
By 1834, the dissatisfied voters in North Carolina were ready to switch their loyalty to a new American political party. They looked to the Whig Party that had formed in the United States. Members of the Whig Party favored banks and improvements such as roads and canals.

Jackson's supporters changed the name of their party to Democrat. They wanted to show that they represented the will of the people. The Whigs and the Democrats began a 20-year rivalry in North Carolina. It led to great progress in the state.

2. In your own words, explain why the Whig Party found supporters in North Carolina.

_____

_____

Demands of the west

Most North Carolina Whigs lived in the west. They supported the reforms that Archibald Murphey had suggested, and wanted the state constitution to be reformed. They threatened the easterners with revolution if this did not happen.

David L. Swain became governor of North Carolina in 1832. He supported the cause of the west. In 1834, he urged the legislature to call a convention to change the 1776 constitution.

3. **DRAW YOUR ANSWER** Draw a map of North Carolina that shows where most Whigs lived.

The 1835 constitutional convention

The convention's delegates met on June 4, 1835. Delegates proposed several changes to the state constitution. The Senate would have 50 members, based on taxes paid per district. This gave the east more representation. The House of Commons would have 120 members, based on population. This gave the west more representation. Catholics were allowed to hold public office. In the new constitution, free African men lost the right to vote.

The convention of 1835 gave people from both east and west a role in government and state policies. It also set the stage for improvements in the state.

4. In your own words, explain one positive change and one negative change caused by the convention of 1835.

_____

_____

LOOk Cl⊕ser

🖉 Mark It Up!

5. This painting shows Andrew Jackson, who was elected president in 1828.
   - **Circle** one object in the painting that shows Jackson's military background.
   - **Write** three words or phrases that describe how Jackson appears in the painting.

_____

_____

SECTION
1

Progress and Its Impact on Different Groups

For use with pages 301–307

Before, You Learned
Calls for reform led to a new political party and a new state constitution.

Now You Will Learn
North Carolina's economy grew due to new railroad lines and the gold rush. The state was then able to build schools and help those in need.

Preview Terms & Names

- **Wilmington & Weldon Railroad:** longest railroad in 1840
- **Raleigh & Gaston Railroad:** first interstate railroad in the country
- **North Carolina gold rush:** first gold rush in American history, beginning in 1799
- **Dorothea Dix:** social reformer who lobbied for the welfare of the mentally ill

Take Notes as You Read

1.

Selecting Important Details		
Railroads and gold mining	**Help for the poor and the mentally ill**	**First public schools**
• The first railroad was built in 1840. • Railroads improved trade, communication, and the economy.	• •	• •

The "iron horse" in North Carolina; The Wilmington & Weldon Railroad

The election of 1836 began a long period of Whig-controlled government in the state. It was a time of great progress.

The people of North Carolina became interested in building railroads in the late 1820s and early 1830s. Railroads allowed for faster, easier transportation for people and goods.

The Wilmington & Weldon Railroad was completed in 1840. It ran between Wilmington and Weldon. Although the railroad was a great improvement, it was not very comfortable for passengers.

The first interstate railroad; Connections by rail

Except for a break at the Roanoke River, the Raleigh & Gaston Railroad connected the state capitals of North Carolina and Virginia.

The General Assembly chartered the North Carolina Railroad Company. As a result, trade and communication grew, the economy improved, and pride and patriotism spread.

2. In your own words, explain one benefit of North Carolina's first railroads.

_____

_____

The North Carolina gold rush begins

The North Carolina gold rush, which began in 1799, was the first gold rush in the United States. Early gold miners collected gold in creek beds and surface deposits. Then, in 1825, "lodes" or veins of gold were found deep underground. Lode mines began to open throughout the Piedmont.

Consequences of the gold rush

Wealth from gold mining funded many new businesses. New workers moved into the Piedmont, including native North Carolinians, immigrants, and enslaved Africans. The workers brought new skills, such as using steam engines to pump groundwater out of the mines. Steam engines were soon used to run machines.

3. **DRAW YOUR ANSWER** Draw a picture that shows lode mines.

Establishment of public schools; Defects in the educational system

In January 1839, the General Assembly passed the state's first public school law. It established a primary school in each district. The first school opened on January 20, 1840. However, some counties were not supportive of public schools. As a result, schools varied in quality.

Help for the unfortunate

Under the Whigs, the state began to provide services for people with physical challenges, mental disabilities, the elderly, and invalids. In 1831, the Assembly voted to create poorhouses, places where poor people could live. In 1848, social reformer Dorothea Dix convinced the legislature to fund special hospitals for people with mental illnesses.

4. In your own words, explain why some of the first public schools were better than others.

_____

_____

LOOk Cl⊕ser

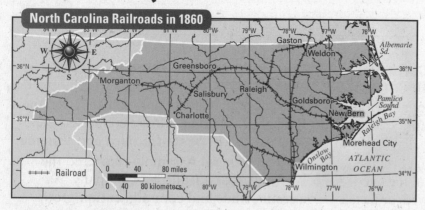

North Carolina Railroads in 1860

✐ Mark It Up!

5. This map shows the railroad lines and terminals in North Carolina in 1860.
   - **Trace** the railroad line that connects the cities of Wilmington and Weldon.
   - **Underline** the two cities with railroad stops and access to ports.

   - **Which** region of the state had more railroads in 1860: the east or the west?

   _____

SECTION 2
The End of the Whig Party
For use with pages 308–311

Before, You Learned
North Carolina's economy grew due to new railroad lines and the gold rush. The state built schools and helped those in need.

Now You Will Learn
An era of progress brought more voting rights, better schools, and prosperity.

Preview Terms & Names

- **Charles Manley:** last Whig governor of North Carolina
- **William W. Holden:** urged the Democratic Party to improve life for common people
- **David S. Reid:** Democrat who ran for governor against Charles Manly in 1848
- **manhood suffrage:** the right of white males to vote even if they did not own property

Take Notes as You Read

CHAPTER 13

1.

Selecting Important Details	
Voting Rights	**Public Education**
• In 1857, the manhood suffrage amendment gave voting rights to 50,000 white males who did not own property.	• 1852:
• Effect on government:	• Effect on schools:

Changes in the Democratic Party
Though the first three Whig governors helped make North Carolina one of the most progressive states in the nation, the fourth Whig governor, Charles Manly, was unimpressive. Manly played a role in bringing about the end of the Whig Party in North Carolina.

Young men joined the Democratic Party and began to change its program. They favored railroads, public education, and giving voting rights to more citizens. One of these men, William W. Holden, urged the Democratic Party to adopt a program that would benefit the common people.

Democratic support for suffrage
In 1848, Democrat David S. Reid ran for governor against the Whig candidate, Charles Manly. At the time, only white males who owned at least 50 acres of land could vote. Reid supported manhood suffrage, or the right of white males to vote even if they did not own property. Manly reacted to Reid's strong stance on suffrage by opposing manhood suffrage.

2. Explain how manhood suffrage would change voting in North Carolina.

_____

_____

Copyright © by McDougal Littell, a division of Houghton Mifflin Company

Failure of the Whig Party; Victory for the Democrats

Manly's stand against manhood suffrage was the beginning of the end of the Whig Party. He barely won the election. Manhood suffrage grew popular throughout the state. The Whig Party declined.

In 1850, Reid beat Manly and became governor. That year, the legislature passed Reid's suffrage amendment, but two years later, when it had to be voted on again, it was defeated. The bill was finally passed in 1857. It gave voting rights to 50,000 more men in North Carolina, making the Senate more responsive to people's needs.

3. In your own words, explain how Charles Manly's reaction to Reid's support of manhood suffrage affected the Whig Party.

_____

_____

Improvement of public education; Schools of higher learning

Public education improved under the Democrats. In 1852, the public school system was reorganized and the office of Superintendent of Common Schools was created to help raise money for schools, set up teacher training, create courses that all schools would teach, and collect progress reports.

During this period, North Carolinians also became more interested in higher education. Schools sponsored by religious denominations opened.

Effectiveness of the reforms

North Carolina's reforms led to greater wealth and prosperity, a successful public school system, and a more representative state government.

4. **DRAW YOUR ANSWER** Draw a picture that shows the effect of reform.

LOOk Clser

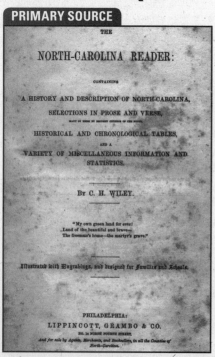

PRIMARY SOURCE

THE

NORTH-CAROLINA READER:

CONTAINING

A HISTORY AND DESCRIPTION OF NORTH-CAROLINA,

SELECTIONS IN PROSE AND VERSE,

HISTORICAL AND CHRONOLOGICAL TABLES,

AND A

VARIETY OF MISCELLANEOUS INFORMATION AND STATISTICS.

By C. H. WILEY.

"My own green land for ever!
Land of the beautiful and brave—
The freeman's home—the martyr's grave."

Illustrated with Engravings, and designed for Families and Schools.

PHILADELPHIA:
LIPPINCOTT, GRAMBO & CO.

Mark It Up!

5. **Read** the primary source document.
   - **Reread** the words that appear in capital letters.
   - **Write** the words that tell what's found inside the reader.

_____

_____

_____

_____

   - **Underline** the short poem that describes North Carolina.

SECTION 1

The Widening Split

For use with pp. 319–324

Before, You Learned
The Whig Party in North Carolina ended mostly because it did not support manhood suffrage.

Now You Will Learn
As new states entered the Union, the North and the South argued over slavery.

Preview Terms & Names

- **Missouri Compromise:** allowed Missouri to enter the Union as a slave state
- **annexation:** addition
- **abolition:** an end to slavery
- **slave codes:** forbade educating enslaved Africans and kept them from leaving their owner's land without permission

Take Notes as You Read

1.

The Missouri Compromise	
Causes:	**Effects:**
• Missouri wanted to enter the Union as a slave state.	•
• Northerners did not want slavery to spread.	•
•	
	•

Spanning a continent
President Polk wanted the Republic of Texas and the Oregon Country to join the United States.

- Mexico claimed Texas, so Polk had to challenge the Mexican government.
- Great Britain claimed Oregon, but Polk wanted to take it without going to war.
- In 1846, the United States and Great Britain divided the Oregon Country.
- Mexico refused to sell California and the New Mexico territory to the United States.

- Polk sent troops into lands claimed by both Mexico and Texas. This started the Mexican-American War.

2. In your own words, describe the main conflict President Polk faced.

_____

_____

CHAPTER 14

A delicate balance

By the 1800s, the North and the South disagreed over slavery. Southerners wanted slavery to be legal in the new western lands. Northerners disagreed.

In 1818, the Missouri Territory asked to enter the Union as a slave state. This request caused a dispute between the North and the South. Senator Henry Clay created the Missouri Compromise to satisfy both the North and the South. Missouri entered the Union as a slave state. Maine had been part of Massachusetts, which entered as a free state. Congress also drew an imaginary line to show where slavery would be allowed in new states.

3. **DRAW YOUR ANSWER** Draw a picture that represents the disagreement over slavery.

The growing crisis

The North and the South disagreed over the treatment of slaves. Some Southerners argued that slavery was "a good." Many Northerners believed that slaves should be given basic human rights.

Southern states responded by passing slave codes that restricted slaves' actions. By the 1850s, most Northerners supported abolition, or an end to slavery.

4. How did the North and the South differ on the subject of slavery?

   _____

   _____

LOOk Cl●ser

New States and the Missouri Compromise

0   250   500 kilometers
Azimuthal Equal-Area Projection

- Free state
- Slave state
- New state between 1820 and 1850
- Missouri Compromise Line, 1820

🖊 Mark It Up!

5. The map shows slave states and free states. It also shows when new states entered the Union. **Reread** the section called "A Delicate Balance."
   - **Circle** the free state that entered the Union in 1820.
   - **Locate** the Missouri Compromise Line.
   - **Write** the letter *S* on the side of the line that allowed slavery.

CHAPTER 14

SECTION 2

The Failure of Compromise

For use with pp. 325–329

Before, You Learned
As new states entered the Union, the North and the South argued over slavery.

Now You Will Learn
Threats of secession and increasing violence made it more difficult for the North and the South to agree about slavery.

Preview Terms & Names

- **Henry Clay:** created the Compromise of 1850
- **secede:** to leave
- **fugitive slave law:** a law that forced people to return runaway slaves
- **Frederick Douglass and Sojourner Truth:** escaped slaves who protested slavery

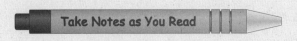
Take Notes as You Read

1.

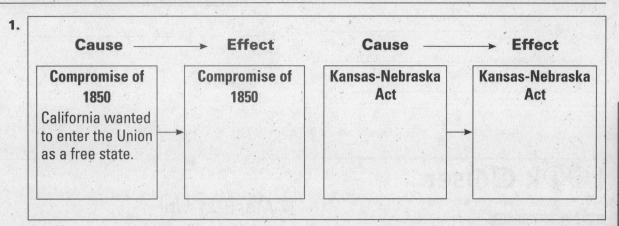

Cause	→	Effect	Cause	→	Effect
Compromise of 1850 California wanted to enter the Union as a free state.		Compromise of 1850	Kansas-Nebraska Act		Kansas-Nebraska Act

The Compromise of 1850

In 1850, California asked to enter the Union as a free state. This would upset the balance of free and slave states. Senator Henry Clay proposed the Compromise of 1850. It stated that California could enter as a free state, and New Mexico and Utah could decide that issue for themselves. Further, slaves could not be bought or sold in the nation's capital, and a stronger fugitive slave law would force the return of runaway slaves.

2. Why was the 1850 Compromise proposed?

_____

_____

Secession; The voice of abolition

Nine slave states met to discuss secession from the Union. They put off the matter because they expected Congress to protect slavery.

Some Northerners did not obey the Fugitive Slave Act. These abolitionists opposed slavery. Some helped slaves escape from the South. The route they took was known as the Underground Railroad.

3. **DRAW YOUR ANSWER** Draw a symbol of the Underground Railroad.

CHAPTER 14

The Kansas-Nebraska Act

In 1854, Senator Stephen A. Douglas proposed the Kansas-Nebraska Act.

- Douglas suggested that Kansas and Nebraska decide the slavery issue by voting, or popular sovereignty.
- The Missouri Compromise was repealed.
- Abolitionists and proslavery Southerners fought one another to prevail in Kansas.
- The fighting spread to Congress in 1856.

4. In your own words, explain the *cause* of the battle over Kansas.

_____

_____

_____

The Know-Nothing Party; The Republican Party

The Kansas-Nebraska Act outraged many Northerners. It also divided the Whig Party.

The "Know-Nothing" party developed in the 1840s. It opposed slavery. It soon fell apart over the slavery issue.

In 1854, some former Whigs created the Republican Party. It also opposed slavery. However, its members did not always agree on what they wanted. Still by 1856, the Republicans had become the major party to oppose the Democrats.

5. Why was the Republican Party created?

_____

_____

LOOk Cl⊕ser

PRIMARY SOURCE

AN
ADDRESS
TO THE PEOPLE OF
NORTH CAROLINA,
ON THE EVILS OF
SLAVERY.

BY
The friends of
LIBERTY AND EQUALITY.

"Anne, liceat invitos in servitutem dare."—DR. PICKARD.
"Not only the Christian religion, but nature herself cries out against a state of slavery :"—POPE LEO. X.

WILLIAM SWAIM PRINTER,
Greensborough, N. C.
1830.

✎ Mark It Up!

6. Read the primary source quotation.
- **Circle** the name of the group that wrote the pamphlet.
- **Underline** the date the pamphlet was printed.
- **Draw** an arrow next to the name of the people to whom the pamphlet is addressed.

SECTION 3

Breaking the Bonds of Union

For use with pp. 330–333

Before, You Learned
The North and the South continued to disagree about slavery.

Now You Will Learn
South Carolina led the march of Southern states out of the Union. They formed a new nation called the Confederate States of America.

Preview Terms & Names

- ***Dred Scott* v. *Sandford:*** legal decision that those of African descent had no constitutional rights
- **Daniel Worth:** a minister who opposed slavery and preached to slaves
- **Harpers Ferry:** Virginia town where John Brown started a slave rebellion
- **arsenal:** a place for storing weapons

Take Notes as You Read

1.

The Election of 1860	
Causes:	**Effects:**
• The Republican Party chose Abraham Lincoln as its candidate for president. •	• • Southern states formed the Confederate States of America.

Thunderbolt from the Supreme Court
On March 6, 1857, the Supreme Court decided the case of *Dred Scott* v. *Sandford.* Two enslaved Africans, Dred and Harriet Scott, sued for their freedom because their owners lived in free territories. The Court decided:

- People of African descent were not citizens under the Constitution.
- Africans could not sue in federal courts.
- Enslaved Africans were "property."
- Congress could not ban slavery.
- The Missouri Compromise was unconstitutional.

Adding fuel to the fire
Also in 1857, Hinton Rowan Helper wrote a book arguing against slavery. He stated that slaves took jobs away from poor whites in the South. Southerners banned the book.

2. Why would the South be pleased with the *Dred Scott* decision?

_____

_____

CHAPTER 14

Bringing abolition south

In 1857, Daniel Worth became a minister in North Carolina. He opposed slavery and preached about his views.

In 1859, John Brown seized a federal arsenal in Harpers Ferry, Virginia. He tried to start a slave rebellion, but was arrested by federal troops. After this, Daniel Worth was arrested for inciting enslaved Africans. He escaped to the North.

A Republican in the White House

In 1860, Abraham Lincoln ran for president. He was part of the new Republican Party, which opposed slavery. After his victory, Southern states began to secede. They formed the Confederate States of America.

3. In your own words, explain why Southern states seceded after the election of 1860.

_____

_____

Reactions in North Carolina

North Carolina did not rush to secede because it was not a strong slaveholding state. However, events soon led to the start of the Civil War.

- On April 12, 1861, South Carolina soldiers fired on federal troops at Fort Sumter.
- Lincoln called for the Union to supply troops for the U.S. Army.
- Both the North and the South formed armies.
- North Carolina became the last Southern state to leave the Union.

4. **DRAW YOUR ANSWER** Draw a symbol that represents the start of the Civil War.

LOOk Closer

The Nation Divides, 1861

Mark It Up!

5. This map shows Union states, Confederate states, and territories in 1861. It also shows slave states and free states.
   - **Reread** the section "Reactions in North Carolina."
   - **Underline** the state where the first shots of the Civil War were fired.
   - **Circle** the two southernmost Union slave states.

CHAPTER 14

SECTION 1

Comparing Advantages
For use with pages 339–341

Before, You Learned

The Southern states formed a new nation: the Confederate States of America.

Now You Will Learn

The North and the South had resources that gave them certain advantages at the start of the Civil War.

Preview Terms & Names

- **Robert E. Lee:** general who was commander of the Confederate army
- **draft:** requiring citizens to sign up for military service
- **Clara Barton:** Civil War nurse who founded the American Red Cross

Take Notes as You Read

1.

COMPARING AND CONTRASTING		
	North	**South**
Advantages	• larger population •	• •
Role of African Americans	•	• Few African Americans served in the army.

Union resources

At the start of the Civil War, the Union's resources were superior to that of the Confederacy. The Union had

- an experienced federal government;
- trade links with foreign nations;
- 23 states (the Confederacy had 11);
- twice the population of the Confederacy;
- most of the nation's factories and mills used to produce war supplies; and
- better roads, canals, and railroads for transportation of goods and soldiers.

Confederate advantages

The Confederacy had fewer resources than the Union. However, it had some advantages:

- General Robert E. Lee was considered the nation's best military leader and he eventually led the Confederate army.
- It was defending itself on familiar land.
- Its soldiers were fighting for their homes, land, and loved ones.

2. In your own words, explain one advantage that each side had going into the war.

_____

_____

CHAPTER 15

Gathering armies

At the beginning of the war, both sides had more than enough soldiers. As the war dragged on, both sides had to draft soldiers. Men between the ages of 18 and 35 had to sign up for military service. However, not everyone was required to serve.

- Rich men on both sides could be excused from the draft.
- African Americans did not serve until late in the war. Many served in the Union; few served in the Confederacy.
- Some women disguised as men became soldiers. Others were scouts or spies.
- Over 3,000 women served as nurses.

3. In your own words, explain one role that women played in the Civil War.

_____

_____

North Carolina's share of troops

North Carolina sent a number of troops, equal to nearly one-fifth of its total white population, to serve as soldiers for the Confederacy. These troops made up about one-sixth of the Confederate army. During the war, North Carolina lost about 40,000 men, more than any other state in the Confederacy.

4. **DRAW YOUR ANSWER** Draw a picture that represents the portion of the Confederate army that was made up of soldiers from North Carolina.

LOOK Closer

Resources of the North and the South, 1860

	North	South
Population	22,700,000	9,000,000*
Railroad (miles)	21,700	9,000
Value of manufacturers	$1,000,000,000	$156,000,000
Corn (bushels per year)	717,000,000	316,000,000
Iron (tons per year)	480, 000	31,000

* Including 3,500,000 enslaved persons

Mark It Up!

5. This table compares the resources that the North and the South had in 1860.
   - **Circle** the total tons of iron produced by the South in 1860.
   - **Underline** the name of the resource that affected each side's transportation.
   - **Identify** the side with more resources in 1860.

CHAPTER 15

SECTION
2

On the Battlefield
For use with pages 342–349

Before, You Learned
Both the North and the South had certain advantages going into the Civil War.

Now You Will Learn
The Union used blockades and other strategies to defeat the Confederacy and end the Civil War.

Preview Terms & Names

- **Anaconda Plan:** plan to stop trade in the South
- **Ulysses S. Grant:** Union general who led the attack against Vicksburg, Mississippi
- **Battle of Antietam:** single bloodiest day of the war
- **Emancipation Proclamation:** freed all slaves in the Confederate states
- **Battle of Gettysburg:** one of the war's costliest battles

Take Notes as You Read

1.

COMPARING AND CONTRASTING		
	North	**South**
Battle Victories	• Battle of Gettysburg •	• •
Effects of Emancipation Proclamation	• Slaves were not freed in Union states.	•

The First Battle of Manassas

The Union planned to blockade all Southern ports and take control of the Mississippi River. This would stop all overseas trade in the South. Newspapers called this the Anaconda Plan, after the snake that squeezes its prey to death.

The First Battle of Manassas was the first major battle of the war. Union forces expected to win easily, but Confederate troops stopped them.

The blockade tightens; War in the East

In April 1862, Union forces captured New Orleans, the South's most important port.

Troops led by General Ulysses S. Grant tried to gain control of the Mississippi River.

In the summer of 1862, General Robert E. Lee planned to invade the North, but a Union soldier discovered his battle plans. Union troops met Lee's army at the Battle of Antietam. Neither side won, but Lee retreated to Virginia.

2. In your own words, explain the purpose of the Anaconda Plan.

_____

_____

CHAPTER 15

The Emancipation Proclamation; Political developments during the war

President Lincoln issued the Emancipation Proclamation. It freed slaves in Confederate states. Ending slavery became a purpose of the war.

Many people opposed the war. In the North, the war split the Democratic Party. In the South, people in northwestern Virginia formed West Virginia, which joined the Union.

War continues in the East and West

Lee invaded the North in 1863. On July 1, Union forces met Lee's troops near Gettysburg, Pennsylvania. The Battle of Gettysburg lasted three days, and the Union won.

General Grant took Vicksburg, Mississippi, giving the Union control of the Mississippi River. Grant and General William T. Sherman then defeated Confederate troops at the Battle of Chattanooga.

Grant takes command; Elections of 1864

In March 1864, Lincoln named Grant commander in chief of all the Union armies. Grant used "total war" to destroy the South's fields, factories, and army. In the West, General Sherman took control of Atlanta, Georgia. This victory helped get Lincoln reelected as president.

Sherman's march to the sea; The end of the war; Lincoln's assassination

Sherman continued to use total war to destroy the South. On April 1, 1865, Lee retreated and the Confederate government fell. The South officially surrendered on April 9, 1865.

On April 14, John Wilkes Booth shot and killed President Lincoln. Vice President Andrew Johnson, a Southerner, became the new president.

3. Explain the final events of the Civil War.

_____

_____

LOOk Closer

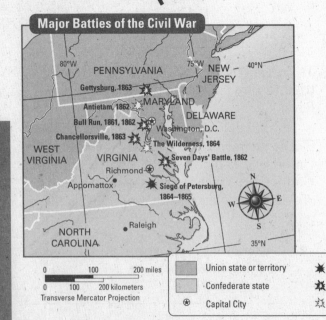

Major Battles of the Civil War

80°W PENNSYLVANIA 75°W NEW 40°N
JERSEY
Gettysburg, 1863
Antietam, 1862 MARYLAND
Bull Run, 1861, 1862 DELAWARE
Chancellorsville, 1863 Washington, D.C.
WEST The Wilderness, 1864
VIRGINIA VIRGINIA Seven Days' Battle, 1862
Richmond
Appomattox Siege of Petersburg,
1864–1865
N
W E
NORTH S
Raleigh
CAROLINA 35°N

0   100   200 miles
0   100   200 kilometers
Transverse Mercator Projection

Union state or territory   Union victory
Confederate state   Confederate victory
Capital City   Indecisive battle

Mark It Up!

4. This map shows the locations of major Civil War battles. It also shows which side won each battle.
   - **Circle** the location of the Battle of Gettysburg.
   - **Draw** an arrow to the year when the Battle of Antietam was fought.
   - **Identify** which side won the Battle of Chancellorsville.

_____

CHAPTER 15

SECTION 3 — North Carolina in the Civil War

For use with pages 352–359

Before, You Learned
The Union used blockades and other strategies to defeat the Confederacy.

Now You Will Learn
North Carolina made important contributions to the Confederacy during the war while defending its rights as a state.

Preview Terms & Names

- **Zebulon B. Vance:** Conservative governor elected in 1862
- *Albemarle*: iron-clad warship used to drive Union forces out of Plymouth
- **Fort Fisher:** fort that protected the port of Wilmington
- **Battle of Bentonville:** Sherman defeated Confederate troops in North Carolina

Take Notes as You Read

1.

COMPARING AND CONTRASTING		
	North Carolina	**Other Confederate States**
Secession	• •	• supported secession • accepted Confederate authority
Sherman's March	•	• Sherman used total war to destroy cities on his march

Preparing for war; Wartime politics in North Carolina

Many North Carolinians accepted the idea of secession. They prepared to defend their state and began making war supplies.

The Democratic Party in North Carolina split in two. The Confederates accepted the loss of state authority in support of the Confederacy. The Conservatives felt state authority was greater than the Confederacy's.

Governor Zebulon B. Vance defends North Carolina's rights

Zebulon B. Vance, a Conservative, was elected governor in 1862. Under his

leadership, the state provided more supplies and soldiers to the Confederacy than any other state.

Vance defended North Carolina against Confederate authority. He refused to suspend habeas corpus and opposed the draft. President Davis did not trust Vance and appointed very few North Carolinians to posts in the Confederate government.

2. Explain the difference between Confederates and Conservatives.

_____

_____

CHAPTER 15

The fighting Tar Heels; Eastern North Carolina is occupied

Troops from North Carolina played key roles in many Confederate victories. General Lee gave them the nickname "Tar Heels" because they did not retreat from battle.

North Carolina threatened the Union plan for a blockade. In February 1862, Union forces captured Roanoke Island and raided towns in eastern North Carolina.

The *Albemarle*; The "Gibraltar of the South"

In 1864, Confederates tried to drive Union forces out of Plymouth using a new iron-clad ship, the *Albemarle*. They succeeded for a time, but the *Albemarle* was eventually destroyed by the Union navy.

Lee depended on the port of Wilmington for supplies. The port was defended by Fort Fisher, known as "the Gibraltar of the South." Fort Fisher finally fell in January 1865.

Sherman in North Carolina; The devastation of North Carolina

The loss of Fort Fisher ended Confederate power in North Carolina and hurt the Confederacy. Without supplies from Wilmington, Lee could not defend Richmond.

When Sherman crossed into North Carolina, he did not use total war because he knew that many North Carolinians were loyal to the Union. Sherman defeated Confederate troops at the Battle of Bentonville. It was the bloodiest battle fought in North Carolina.

The Civil War brought enormous suffering to the people of North Carolina. Food and supplies were scarce, and many buildings were destroyed. Worse, thousands of young men had died.

3. **DRAW YOUR ANSWER** Draw a symbol that represents one effect of the Civil War on the people of North Carolina.

LOOk Closer

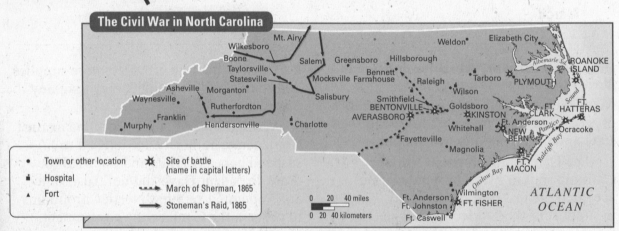

The Civil War in North Carolina

Mark It Up!

4. This map shows the locations of major events in the Civil War in North Carolina.
   • **Underline** the name of the fort that protected the port of Wilmington.

   • **Circle** the site of the Battle of Bentonville.
   • **Identify** where most battles took place.

SECTION 1

Restoring the Union
For use with pages 365–367

Before, You Learned
North Carolina made important contributions to the Confederacy during the Civil War. It also defended its rights as a state.

Now You Will Learn
President Johnson did not strictly enforce his plan for Reconstruction.

Preview Terms & Names

- **Reconstruction:** the process of rebuilding the Southern states after the Civil War
- **Andrew Johnson:** president after Lincoln was killed
- **Thirteenth Amendment:** passed in 1865; outlawed slavery in the United States
- **Black Codes:** laws that strictly limited the freedom of formerly enslaved people

Take Notes as You Read

1.

SUMMARIZING		
Main Idea		**Summary**
• After becoming president, Johnson made his plan for Reconstruction.	⇒	Thirteenth Amendment:
• Many members of Congress thought Johnson was not punishing the South enough.	⇒	Black Codes:

Copyright © by McDougal Littell, a division of Houghton Mifflin Company

Lincoln's plan for Reconstruction
Two years before the end of the war, President Lincoln developed a plan for the Reconstruction, or rebuilding, of the Southern states so they could quickly rejoin the Union.

Lincoln announced his plan on December 8, 1863. The Proclamation of Amnesty and Reconstruction fully pardoned most Southerners involved in the war.

Southerners had to swear their loyalty to the Constitution. They also had to agree to end slavery. When enough citizens in a Confederate state made these promises and the state reorganized its government, it could return to the Union.

Johnson supports Lincoln's plan
After Lincoln was assassinated, Andrew Johnson became president. Under his plan for Reconstruction, new state governments had to write new constitutions and approve the Thirteenth Amendment, which outlawed slavery. Johnson did not look closely at the new governments. Mississippi entered the Union, but it did not ratify, or approve, the Thirteenth Amendment.

2. Explain the main problem with Johnson's plan for Reconstruction.

_____

_____

CHAPTER 16

North Carolina and Johnson's plan

Johnson chose W. W. Holden to be provisional governor of North Carolina until the state could rejoin the Union. Holden supported the president's plan for Reconstruction. Holden held a convention in October 1865. The convention made several changes. It

- ended the Ordinance of Secession;
- abolished slavery in North Carolina;
- planned an election for governor, legislators, and congressmen; and
- decided not to pay the state's war debts.

Holden lost the race for governor to Jonathan Worth, a former Whig and Unionist.

3. In your own words, explain two changes made by Governor Holden's convention.

_____

_____

Anger over Black Codes

Many members of Congress were upset with the way Johnson handled Reconstruction. They felt that the South was not being punished enough.

Southern states passed Black Codes—laws that strictly limited the freedom of formerly enslaved people. Under these laws, African Americans could not own guns or meet after sunset. They could be put in prison if they did not have jobs, and some states limited the kinds of work African Americans could do.

Many members of Congress felt that if such laws were allowed, the Civil War had accomplished nothing.

4. **DRAW YOUR ANSWER** Draw a picture that represents one effect of Black Codes.

LOOk Closer

PRIMARY SOURCE

In his Second Inaugural Address, President Lincoln asked Americans "to bind up the nation's wounds . . . to do all which may achieve and cherish a just and lasting peace among ourselves and with all nations."

President Lincoln

Mark It Up!

5. Read the primary source quotation.
   - **Circle** the event at which Lincoln spoke these words.
   - **Underline** words that describe Lincoln's goal for the Union.
   - **Write** a sentence explaining what Lincoln asked Americans to do.

_____

_____

SECTION 2

Congress Takes Over
For use with pages 368–370

Before, You Learned
President Johnson did not strictly enforce his plan for Reconstruction.

Now You Will Learn
Unhappy with Johnson's plan, Republicans took control of Congress and placed Southern states under military control.

Preview Terms & Names

- **Freedmen's Bureau:** a federal agency set up to help people in the South
- **Fourteenth Amendment:** made African Americans citizens of the United States
- **Fifteenth Amendment:** declared that the right to vote cannot be denied due to race, color, or having been a slave

Take Notes as You Read

1.

SUMMARIZING

Main Idea	Summary
• President Johnson and Congress clashed over plans for Reconstruction.	The Fourteenth Amendment:
• President Grant worked with Republicans in Congress to give rights to African Americans.	The Fifteenth Amendment:

The extension of the Freedmen's Bureau

Many Republicans in Congress disliked President Johnson's plan for Reconstruction. They wanted to punish former Confederate states, and protect freedmen's rights and give them the right to vote. Radical and moderate Republicans set up the Joint Committee on Reconstruction. It began making a plan to replace Johnson's.

The committee encouraged Congress to pass a new Freedmen's Bureau Bill. The bureau gave food, medicine, and other aid to white and African-American Southerners. It also providing schooling for formerly enslaved people.

The clash between Johnson and Congress

Johnson refused to sign the new Freedmen's Bureau Bill. Johnson wanted local courts, not military courts, to try cases involving civil rights of African Americans. In 1866, Congress passed the Fourteenth Amendment to the Constitution. It gave citizenship to African Americans. Johnson had encouraged Southern states to oppose the amendment.

2. Explain how the Freedmen's Bureau helped people in the South.

_____

_____

CHAPTER 16

Congress in control

With Republicans in control, Congress put the army in charge of the former Confederate states. Before the army could leave, each state had to write a new constitution that gave African-American males voting rights. Each state also had to approve the Fourteenth Amendment.

Johnson vetoed bills passed by Congress and ignored Congress when it overrode his vetoes. In response, Congress voted to impeach him, or charge him with wrongdoing. If found guilty, he would be removed from office. Congress voted, and Johnson remained president by a single vote.

3. In your own words, explain why Congress voted on impeaching President Johnson.

_____

_____

Republican President Ulysses S. Grant

In 1868, the Republicans helped to elect Ulysses S. Grant as president. Then in 1869, Congress passed the Fifteenth Amendment to the Constitution. It declared that states could not deny voting rights due to race, color, or having been a slave.

The conflict over Reconstruction in North Carolina

Congress would not allow North Carolina's senators in Congress. Nevertheless, the General Assembly ratified the Thirteenth Amendment. W. W. Holden helped organize North Carolina's Republican Party in 1867. Still, North Carolina was occupied by federal troops.

4. DRAW YOUR ANSWER Draw a picture that shows the purpose and result of the Fifteenth Amendment.

_____

LOOk Closer

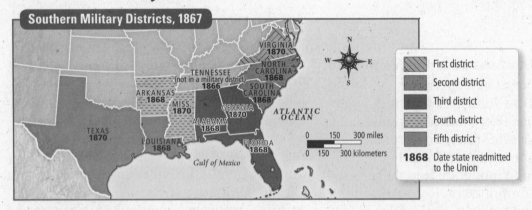

Southern Military Districts, 1867

✎ Mark It Up!

5. This map shows the military districts created by Congress in 1867. It also shows the dates when Southern states were readmitted to the Union.
  • **Circle** the district that included North Carolina.

  • **Underline** the name of the first Southern state readmitted to the Union.

  • In what year did the most Southern states return to the Union?

_____

SECTION 3
The Impact of Reconstruction on North Carolina
For use with pages 371–373

Before, You Learned
The Republican Congress placed Southern states under military control.

Now You Will Learn
The Republican Party gained power in North Carolina, drafted a new constitution and led the state into the Union.

Preview Terms & Names

- **carpetbagger:** insulting nickname for a Northerner who went South during Reconstruction to serve in the government
- **scalawag:** insulting nickname for Southerners in the Republican government
- **Ku Klux Klan:** secret society of ex-Confederates that used intimidation to return power to white males

CHAPTER 16

Take Notes as You Read

1.

SUMMARIZING

Main Idea	Summary
• North Carolina's new state constitution was challenged by some white citizens.	Ku Klux Klan:
• The Republican Party eventually triumphed in North Carolina.	Rejoining the Union:

Newcomers in Southern government

Between 1867 and 1870, all the former Confederate states adopted constitutions that were acceptable to Congress and returned to the Union. However, many white Southerners found their new governments unacceptable.

Reconstruction brought new people into the government. African Americans served in the new governments. Enemies of the new governments had insulting nicknames for the new leaders. Northerners were called carpetbaggers. Many believed they did not truly wish to help the South. Southerners were called scalawags, meaning crooks or traitors.

Changes in state governments

The new Republican state governments started public schools, rebuilt communities, and tried to improve the economy. Southern governments became more democratic, and poor people had larger roles in political life.

2. DRAW YOUR ANSWER Draw a picture that shows one change brought about by new Republican state governments.

CHAPTER 16

Resistance to change

Many white Southerners did not like the changes that came with Reconstruction. Taxes were high. Confederate veterans had no say in government. A few people turned to violence to return power to white men. A group of ex-Confederates formed a secret society known as the Ku Klux Klan. They attacked and killed African Americans and some whites.

A new constitution for North Carolina

North Carolina delegates drafted a new state constitution. It prohibited slavery, established free public schools for all people, and funded railroads and care for the poor. All voters had to register before they could vote on the new constitution.

3. Why did Confederate veterans oppose their new government?

_____

_____

The Klan in North Carolina

The Ku Klux Klan made its first appearance in North Carolina when voting took place for the new constitution. State and county elections were held at the same time. Klan members tried to scare African-American voters. Nevertheless, the Republicans won a clear victory, and W. W. Holden was elected governor.

The return of North Carolina to the Union

Holden's followers quickly ratified the Fourteenth Amendment and elected two Republican senators. North Carolina's Assembly was finally allowed to meet. On July 20, 1868, North Carolina returned to the Union.

4. In your own words, explain why the Ku Klux Klan appeared in North Carolina.

_____

_____

LOOk Closer

Mark It Up!

5. This illustration shows African Americans voting soon after they gained suffrage. It represents three groups of voters.
- **Circle** the man who represents voters who were formerly enslaved.
- **Draw** an arrow to the man who represents wealthy voters.
- **Write** the letter *S* on the man who represents voters who were soldiers.

SECTION 4

The End of Reconstruction
For use with pages 374–377

Before, You Learned
The Republican Party drafted a new state constitution and led the state back to the Union.

Now You Will Learn
Conservatives took control of North Carolina's government as Reconstruction came to an end in the state.

Preview Terms & Names

- **Wyatt Outlaw:** African-American Republican leader murdered by the Ku Klux Klan
- **John W. Stephens:** white Republican leader murdered by the Ku Klux Klan
- **George W. Kirk:** leader of militia that arrested suspected Ku Klux Klan members
- **Rutherford B. Hayes:** president who ended Reconstruction

Take Notes as You Read

1.

SUMMARIZING

Main Idea		Summary
• Conservatives in North Carolina opposed the Republican government.	→	The Klan:
• Conservatives gained control, bringing "home rule" and with it, an end to Reconstruction in the state.	→	Zebulon B. Vance:

The spread of terror in North Carolina
Under Governor Holden, some government officials and Republican businessmen used bribery and fraud to become rich. Conservatives turned to the Ku Klux Klan to regain control of state government. The Klan frightened, hurt, and even killed people to keep them from voting for Republicans. Within a few months, Republicans lost control of 13 counties.

As the 1870 election neared, the Klan's terrorism increased. Republican leaders Wyatt Outlaw and John W. Stephens were murdered by the Klan in early 1870.

The Kirk-Holden War
The General Assembly passed an act that allowed the governor to place counties under martial law if life and property were in danger. Colonel George W. Kirk led a militia that arrested more than 100 men suspected of being Klan members. Kirk's actions violated the Fourteenth Amendment, so a federal judge ordered most of the prisoners freed.

2. Explain why Conservatives opposed the government under Holden.

_____

_____

CHAPTER 16

The Conservatives in control

Conservatives in the Assembly voted to impeach Holden. He was convicted and removed from office in 1871. In 1875, delegates passed amendments that restored power to the legislature. Many in the state rejoiced that "home rule" had been restored.

The impact of Reconstruction on North Carolina

African Americans were able to own land, start businesses, educate themselves, and participate in government. Poor white citizens began to take part in government. North Carolina adopted a constitution that granted universal manhood suffrage.

3. In your own words, explain one way that Reconstruction helped African Americans.

_____

_____

Social improvements

During Reconstruction, North Carolina established a required system of universal public education. It also began to provide services for people who were poor, orphaned, or in prison, or who had mental disabilities. The state also encouraged industrial development.

Reconstruction's legacy

By 1876, the United States was united once more. In 1877, President Rutherford B. Hayes withdrew the army from the Southern states. Southerners still suffered from the effects of the war. Many were poor, and farms and businesses did not grow. African Americans lost many of the rights they had gained, and they struggled against discrimination.

4. **DRAW YOUR ANSWER** Draw a picture showing changes during Reconstruction.

_____

LOOk Cl⊕ser

PRIMARY SOURCE

FACTS FOR THE PEOPLE

To Read, Ponder and Digest, if they can.

For the benefit of those who really desire information, and to show in proper light the Extravagance, Wastefulness, and utter disregard for the people's best interests, shown by the Radical party, we submit the following comparison of the expense of one year of Democratic rule, under Gov. Bragg in 1857 & '58 ; and one year ending Sept. 30th, 1869, under the Radical rule of William W. Holden :

✎ Mark It Up!

5. This document was published by Conservatives who opposed the leadership of Republican governor W.W. Holden.
   - **Circle** the audience for whom this document was written.
   - **Write** the name the author gives to Holden's political party.

_____

   - **Underline** the three negative qualities that the document claims to show about Holden's political party.

SECTION 1

The Rise of Industry in the United States

For use with pages 385–389

Before, You Learned

Conservatives gained control of North Carolina's government as Reconstruction ended.

Now You Will Learn

During the Industrial Revolution, two new industries—railroads and steel—grew quickly.

Preview Terms & Names

- **Industrial Revolution:** time when people began manufacturing goods with machines
- **Homestead Act:** gave free land in the West to anyone who would farm it for five years
- **transcontinental railroad:** connected east and west coasts
- **corporation:** business with many owners
- **monopoly:** total control of an industry

Take Notes as You Read

1.

ANALYZING CAUSES AND EFFECTS		
Causes		**Effects**
• Factories began producing steel quickly and cheaply.	→	•
• People discovered that oil could be used to grease and power machinery.	→	•

Railroads lead industrial development

In 1862, Congress passed the Homestead Act, giving free land in the West to anyone who would farm it for five years. Congress also approved the building of the first transcontinental railroad.

Two companies built this railroad, which would connect the east and west coasts. One began building tracks in Nebraska heading west, and the other headed east from San Francisco. On May 10, 1869, the tracks came together. Many companies began building railroads connecting all parts of the nation.

Steel replaces iron

The steel industry grew quickly. Steel is stronger and easier to shape than iron and could be made quickly and cheaply.

Because of steel's new, lower prices, demand for it grew. Railroad companies switched from iron to steel. The man most responsible for the growth of the U.S. steel industry was Andrew Carnegie.

2. In your own words, explain why railroad companies switched from iron to steel.

_____

_____

_____

CHAPTER 17

The growth of corporations

Carnegie bought stocks in corporations, businesses with many owners. In the 1870s, he built the most up-to-date steel mill in the world. As steel became the most important building material, Carnegie became one of the richest men in the world.

The discovery of "black gold"

"Black gold," or oil, was discovered in the United States in the late 1850s. It could be used for lighting lamps and powering machinery, but it first had to be processed. In 1863, John D. Rockefeller started Standard Oil Company, an oil-refining business. Standard Oil soon became a monopoly.

3. DRAW YOUR RESPONSE Draw a symbol that shows how Andrew Carnegie and John D. Rockefeller were alike.

Communicating by wire; Edison's sparks of invention

In 1876, Alexander Graham Bell invented the telephone. Thomas Alva Edison's inventions include the phonograph, motion picture camera, light bulb, and electric power plant.

Ford's new way of manufacturing; Robber barons or captains of industry?

In 1903, Henry Ford set up a car factory where workers used an assembly line and interchangeable parts. By 1927, Ford's factories were producing one car about every 25 seconds.

Industrialists grew very rich. Some saw them as "robber barons" who took advantage of workers and destroyed competitors. Others saw them as "captains of industry." There was truth in both views.

4. Explain why some people saw industrialists as "robber barons."

_____

_____

L👓k Cl⊕ser

Transcontinental Railroads, 1850–1900

🖉 Mark It Up!

5. This map shows the first transcontinental railroad and the four U.S. time zones.

• **Circle** the 8 cities connected by the first transcontinental railroad.

• **Underline** the time zone that you live in.

SECTION 2

Life in the Country and the City

For use with pages 390–392

Before, You Learned

During the Industrial Revolution, two new industries—railroads and steel—grew quickly.

Now You Will Learn

Life changed on farms and in cities due to urbanization and immigration movements in the late 1800s.

Preview Terms & Names

- **urbanization:** the movement of people from rural to urban areas
- **immigration:** the movement of people from overseas to the United States
- **tenement:** crowded city apartment buildings that had tiny rooms and few windows

Take Notes as You Read

1.

ANALYZING CAUSES AND EFFECTS	
Causes	**Effects**
• New farming methods, tools, and machines were developed.	•
•	• American cities had more wealth and jobs, but they also faced overcrowding and poverty.

Industrialization changes American farming; Life on the farm changes

In the late 1800s, farming was changing quickly. New methods, such as crop rotation and the use of fertilizers and pesticides, made farming more productive. Machines such as the steel plow and the tractor made farming easier.

As a result, many farmers could no longer find work in the country. They moved to cities, seeking factory jobs. This movement of people from rural to urban areas is called urbanization.

For those who continued to farm, life improved. Railroads made it easier and

faster to transport supplies. Telephones connected farmers to each other and to cities. Mail service allowed farmers to buy the latest goods from catalogues.

As farming methods and technology continued to improve, however, fewer farmers were needed. Many former farmers continued to move to cities.

2. Explain how tools and machines helped and hurt American farmers.

_____

_____

CHAPTER 17

Immigration fuels industrial growth

Even with ex-farmers moving to factory work, America's industries still did not have enough workers. Between 1865 and 1890, more than 12 million people came to the United States in search of better jobs and a better life. This movement of people is called immigration.

Most immigrants settled in the Northeast and the Midwest, though some settled in the West and the South. Industrial development remained slow in North Carolina and other states in the South. As a result, few jobs were available in these areas.

3. **DRAW YOUR RESPONSE** Draw a map that shows where most immigrants settled in the United States between 1865 and 1890.

Life changes in American cities

Industry brought new wealth and new kinds of jobs to American cities. Many people became factory workers, and others provided services. By 1900, millions were doing jobs that had not existed before 1860.

The flood of new people also brought problems, such as overcrowding and poverty. Many workers lived in tenements, which were apartment buildings with tiny rooms and few windows. Landlords made few improvements or repairs to the buildings.

Middle-class people lived differently. While the wealthiest lived in magnificent mansions, many middle-class families moved to suburbs. Their single-family homes had better plumbing, electricity, telephones, and yards for their enjoyment.

4. How did cities change in the late 1800s?

_____

_____

LOOk Closer

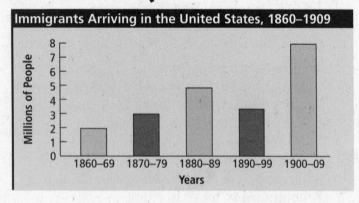

Immigrants Arriving in the United States, 1860–1909

Mark It Up!

5. This graph shows how many millions of immigrants came to the United States during each decade from 1860 to 1909.
   - **Circle** the two decades in which the most immigrants arrived.
   - How many immigrants arrived between 1870 and 1879?

_____

   - How many more immigrants arrived from 1900 to 1909 than from 1860 to 1869?

_____

SECTION 3 | Calls for Reform: Populism and Progressivism

For use with pages 393–397

Before, You Learned
Life changed on farms and in cities in the late 1800s.

Now You Will Learn
Many Americans demanded reforms to solve the problems brought on by industrialization.

Preview Terms & Names

- **inflation:** a rise in prices
- **labor union:** organizations that help workers fight for better working conditions and wages
- **strike:** action in which workers stop working to pressure their employer
- **progressivism:** reform movement that tried to solve problems in America

CHAPTER 17

Take Notes as You Read

1.

ANALYZING CAUSES AND EFFECTS	
Causes	**Effects**
• The government did not help farmers fight unfair business practices.	•
•	• The reform movement known as progressivism began.

The plight of farmers; Farmers take action

Farmers cried out for reform. With more crops available for sale, prices and profits fell. Farmers had to borrow money from banks at high interest rates. They wanted the government to make railroads and banks use fair business practices. Farmers also wanted the government to put more money into circulation so they could charge more for their crops. They believed this could help them pay off their bank loans.

Farmers formed groups to help themselves. The Grange convinced state legislatures to regulate railroad shipping rates. The Farmer's Alliance backed political candidates who shared their goals. In 1892, the Alliance formed the Populist Party.

Populism

Populism supported farmers and working people. Populists wanted the government to control transportation and communication businesses. They also wanted better working conditions, an eight-hour workday, and higher wages for workers.

2. Explain the goal of populism.

_____

_____

The plight of industrial workers

Factory workers worked long hours in dangerous conditions. Many workers joined labor unions to help them bargain for better wages and conditions. Workers could pressure companies by threatening to strike, refusing to work in order to gain better pay and benefits. Businesses tried to prevent workers from joining unions.

City life gets worse; Progressivism

Workers also had to struggle with crime, pollution, and disease. As life in cities got worse, a new reform movement began, known as progressivism. Progressives believed that the government should solve social, economic, and political problems.

3. **DRAW YOUR ANSWER** Draw a symbol that shows one problem progressives wanted to solve.

Reform in city and state government

In the 1870s and 1880s, reformers discovered that government corruption caused many problems faced by poor people. Groups pressured city governments to reduce fire danger and crime. They convinced state governments to give voters more power.

Reform at the national level; A progressive president

In 1890, the Sherman Antitrust Act made it illegal for any company to control an entire industry. However, the law was not enforced. Finally, President Theodore Roosevelt, the first progressive president, began to enforce the act. Progressives continued to work for reforms into the 1920s in areas such as food safety.

4. In your own words, explain the purpose of the Sherman Antitrust Act.

_____

_____

_____

LO☉k Cl⊕ser

✎ Mark It Up!

5. John D. Rockefeller owned Standard Oil Company. In this political cartoon, he snips off the competing rosebuds in order to perfect his own company's flower.
   • **Circle** the part of the plant that represents Standard Oil Company.
   • **Draw** an arrow to the rosebud that represents one competing oil company.
   • **Write** one word that describes how the competitors appear in the cartoon.

   _____

SECTION 1

Industry in North Carolina
For use with pages 405–411

Before, You Learned
As the United States recovered from the Civil War, industrialization began to transform the nation.

Now You Will Learn
Although it came more slowly to the South, the Industrial Revolution brought many changes to daily life.

Preview Terms & Names

- **R. J. Reynolds:** major tobacco producer
- **Washington Duke:** made Durham the most important tobacco center in North Carolina
- **trust:** a business organization that combines all companies in an industry into one business
- **High Point:** home to the first company to make large amounts of furniture in North Carolina

Take Notes as You Read

1.

DRAWING CONCLUSIONS

Event: American Tobacco Company was sued under the Sherman Antitrust Act in 1908.	**Fact:** Railroads brought growth to all industries in North Carolina.
Conclusion:	**Conclusion:**

Industry in North Carolina

The textile industry was one of the first to recover after the war. Old mills were revived and new ones established. Mills and factories used water, then steam, then electricity to power machines. By 1900, North Carolina produced more cotton textiles than any other Southern state except South Carolina.

After the war, demand for tobacco grew. R. J. Reynolds moved to North Carolina and became a major tobacco producer. Washington Duke and his sons made Durham an important tobacco center. In 1881, the Dukes decided to make cigarettes. They began to use rolling machines, which cut costs and produced more cigarettes

that could sell at a lower price. Demand for cigarettes greatly increased.

The Dukes created the American Tobacco Company, and it became the largest tobacco company in the world. In 1911, the company was forced to split into four. The wealthy Dukes made large donations to the college that eventually became Duke University and set up a permanent fund to help other institutions.

2. Explain why American Tobacco Company was forced to split in 1911.

_____

_____

CHAPTER 18

North Carolina's railroads

After the Civil War, many railroads were built in North Carolina. By 1894, the state's railroads had attracted the attention of the most powerful banker in the United States, J. P. Morgan.

Morgan bought the rights to railroads in North Carolina. Soon, the state linked to rail lines that ran from New York to New Orleans and from Jacksonville to Memphis. By 1900, North Carolina had nearly 4,000 miles of rail. Railroads were major factors in the growth of all North Carolina's industries, especially the new, but quickly expanding, furniture industry.

3. **DRAW YOUR RESPONSE** Draw a symbol that shows how a trust controls an industry.

The furniture industry; Towns grow

The first factory to produce large quantities of furniture was started by three men from High Point. In 1889, they started the High Point Manufacturing Company. High Point succeeded because it had good rail transportation, plenty of hardwood forests, and lots of workers. Furniture factories began to spring up all along the North Carolina Railroad.

The building of mills and factories helped towns grow. By 1900, the state had six towns with more than 10,000 people, electricity, running water, streetcars, telephones, and paved streets. However, North Carolina remained mostly rural.

4. Explain how industry affected the growth of towns in North Carolina.

_____

_____

_____

LOOk Closer

Population Density of the United States, 1880

🖉 Mark It Up!

5. This map shows the number of people per square mile in the United States in 1880.
   • **Label** North Carolina on the map.
   • **Circle** the areas in North Carolina that had the most people per square mile in 1880.

   • **Write** the region of the country that had the most people per square mile in 1880.

_____

SECTION 2

Agriculture in North Carolina

For use with pages 412–415

Before, You Learned
The Industrial Revolution brought many changes to daily life.

Now You Will Learn
Like other farmers, North Carolina's farmers struggled after 1865 as their costs rose but selling prices fell.

Preview Terms & Names

- **tenant farming:** a system of farming in which a farmer rents farmland from the landowner
- **sharecropping:** a system of labor in which people worked farms for landowners in exchange for income from the crop

Take Notes as You Read

1.

DRAWING CONCLUSIONS	
Fact: Tenants and sharecroppers lived and worked on land they did not own.	**Fact:** Railroads charged high shipping rates that farmers could not afford.
Conclusion:	**Conclusion:**

Freedmen and freedwomen

Many of the 40,000 men who died in the Civil War had been from farms. The war had also destroyed farms, barns, and homes. The end of slavery changed the system of labor. At the end of the war, 350,000 enslaved African laborers were freed in the state. Some stayed on the farms they had worked before, and a new relationship between employer and worker soon developed.

Tenant farmers and sharecroppers

After the war, many skilled farm workers were left without money or land. Many landowners had land but little money to pay wages. This led to tenant farming and sharecropping.

Under these systems, people lived and worked on farms that belonged to someone else. A tenant rented land, provided the labor, and purchased some equipment and supplies. A sharecropper only provided labor. Both received a share of the income from the crop. Life was difficult for these workers, and their standard of living was low. However, large numbers of landless people were able to meet minimal basic needs.

2. Explain the main difference between tenants and sharecroppers.

_____

_____

Economic factors

The years after the war were made worse by four economic forces that farmers could not control:

- low crop prices
- high cost of supplies
- high land tax
- high interest rates on loans

Progress and changes in crop production

Some farmers switched to growing crops that would bring them a larger profit. They grew cash crops such as cotton and tobacco instead of vegetables, grains, or fruits. Soon, farms were as productive as they had been before the war.

3. In your own words, explain why farmers began growing cotton and tobacco.

_____

_____

Problems with farming; Problems with transportation

New methods and technology produced more crops. As a result, prices of crops fell. This problem became worse in 1873 when the economy went into a sharp decline, or depression. Many sharecroppers and tenant farmers went into debt just to pay their bills.

Farmers also struggled with high shipping rates charged by railroads. They called on the legislature for help. They were ignored, and so they began to organize politically to achieve the reforms.

4. **DRAW YOUR ANSWER** Draw a symbol that represents what happened to crop prices due to new farming methods and technology.

LOOk Closer

Amount of Cotton and Tobacco Produced in North Carolina

Year	Bales of Cotton	Pounds of Tobacco
1860	145,000	33,000,000
1870	145,000	11,000,000
1880	390,000	27,000,000
1890	360,000	36,000,000
1900	460,000	128,000,000

Mark It Up!

5. This chart shows how much cotton and tobacco were produced in North Carolina from 1860 to 1900.
   - **Circle** the amount of tobacco produced in 1880.
   - **Underline** the two years when cotton production remained the same.
   - Did tobacco production increase or decrease from 1860 to 1870?

_____

SECTION 3 — Reform and Reaction in North Carolina

For use with pages 416–421

Before, You Learned
Like other farmers, North Carolina's farmers struggled after 1865 as their costs rose but selling prices fell.

Now You Will Learn
North Carolinians struggled to adjust to changes caused by industrialization and demanded reforms.

Preview Terms & Names

- **Leonidas L. Polk:** spokesman for North Carolina farmers, later commissioner of agriculture in the state
- **Fusion:** an alliance of North Carolina Populists and Republicans
- **Wilmington Race Riot:** incident in which a white mob killed 11 African Americans
- **Prohibition:** banning of alcoholic beverages

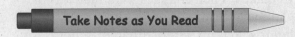
Take Notes as You Read

1.

DRAWING CONCLUSIONS

Event: In 1894, the Fusion alliance took control and gave African Americans more political power.	**Fact:** In 1919, the state increased the school year from four months to six months for students ages 6 to 12.
Conclusion:	**Conclusion:**

The Farmers Alliance in North Carolina; Leonidas L. Polk

As conditions worsened for farmers in the late 1890s, many began to demand government action to help them. When Democratic leaders did not help, farmers decided to help themselves.

Leonidas L. Polk became the most important spokesman for North Carolina farmers in the late 1800s. In 1877, he became the state's first commissioner of agriculture. In 1887, he organized the North Carolina Farmers' Association. He helped start a new college to teach "practical" subjects and demanded regulation of the railroads.

Populism and "Fusion" politics

Polk became president of the National Farmers Alliance in 1889. With his help, the Assembly stopped unfair railroad practices and lowered shipping rates. The Populists decided to join with Republicans. In 1894, this Fusion alliance swept the state elections. They made many reforms and gave African Americans the ability to hold office.

2. Why was the Fusion alliance formed?

_____

_____

CHAPTER 18

Democrats regain control; Progressivism in North Carolina

When Democrats lost at the polls, they called for a return to white power and tried to scare black voters. In 1898, the Democrats regained control of state government. The day after the election, a white mob killed 11 African Americans during the Wilmington Race Riot.

After this incident, progressive Democratic leaders began to believe that separation of the races was necessary for reform. They also fought to take away African Americans' voting rights.

Religion and women in North Carolina; The struggle for woman suffrage

Many women took part in church activities. Some supported progressive reforms including woman suffrage, giving voting rights to women. The North Carolina Assembly, however, voted against woman suffrage when it had a chance to ratify an amendment to the United States Constitution.

Other progressive and educational reforms

In 1908, progressives succeeded in pressuring the Assembly to enact Prohibition, the banning of alcoholic beverages. Their work led to improved working conditions and to the end of child labor. Roads, colleges and universities, and public schools were all improved.

The 1868 state constitution required funding of free public schools that were to stay open six months a year. City schools were able to make more progress than schools in rural places. Then changes were made to the way money was distributed, and rural schools began to catch up. Unfortunately, schools for African Americans did not improve until the 1950s and 1960s.

4. **DRAW YOUR ANSWER** Draw a picture that shows one successful progressive reform.

LOOk Closer

✏ Mark It Up!

5. This photograph shows young workers at the Vivian Cotton Mills in North Carolina.
   - **Circle** the worker who appears to be the youngest.
   - **Write** three words that describe how the workers appear in this photograph.

   _____

   _____

   - **Write** a sentence describing the photograph using the words above.

   _____

   _____

CHAPTER 18

SECTION 1

Becoming a World Power

For use with pages 429–432

Before, You Learned
People in North Carolina adjusted to industrialization and many sought reforms.

Now You Will Learn
By the early 1900s, the United States was one of the richest nations in the world, conducting trade and business in many countries.

Preview Terms & Names

- **Theodore Roosevelt:** led the Rough Riders against Spain to help free Cuba
- **imperialism:** conquering and ruling other lands
- **expansionist:** a person who favored taking over land outside the country
- **Panama Canal:** canal that opened in 1914 connecting the Atlantic and Pacific oceans

Take Notes as You Read

1.

MAKING GENERALIZATIONS

Event: In 1895, U.S. citizens learned about the Cuban revolution by reading newspapers.	**Fact:** The United States wanted to build the Panama Canal to make it easier to trade with Pacific islands.
↓	↓
Generalization:	**Generalization:**

A war with Spain; Victory in Cuba

In 1895, the residents of the island of Cuba, just 90 miles off the coast of Florida, revolted against Spanish rule. When people in the United States learned of the conflict, many urged Congress to help free Cuba.

At first, the United States tried to stay out of the revolution. Then, an American battleship blew up in a Cuban harbor, killing 250 people. The U.S. declared war on Spain.

The United States sent a fleet of battleships to the Philippines, islands in the Pacific ruled by Spain. On May 1, 1898, the fleet captured or destroyed every Spanish ship in the Philippine capital. While fighting continued in the Philippines, more

than 17,000 U.S. soldiers sailed to Cuba. Theodore Roosevelt led the Rough Riders, a group that included cowboys, lumberjacks, and Native Americans. They took over Spanish forts near Santiago, Cuba.

By August 1898, the U.S. had won the war. Spain agreed to free Cuba, turn over the islands of Guam and Puerto Rico, and sell the Philippines to the U.S. for $20 million.

2. Why did the United States become involved in the Cuban revolution?

_____

_____

CHAPTER 19

The debate over the treaty

The United States had to approve the peace treaty with Spain. Some senators favored expanding U.S. territory. Others disagreed. Most Americans favored expansion, though, and the treaty was approved.

Expanding the nation

In 1867, the United States bought Alaska from Russia. Again, people disagreed over expanding the nation. Expansionists won the debate. In 1959, Alaska became the 49th U.S. state.

In 1893, U.S. settlers in Hawaii, a Pacific island, led a revolt. In 1898, Hawaii became a U.S. territory, and in 1959, it became the nation's 50th state.

3. Explain how most Americans in the late 1800s felt about expanding the nation.

_____

_____

A shortcut between oceans; Effects on North Carolina

As trade grew with the Pacific Islands, the United States wanted a faster, safer route through Central America. Many dreamed of a canal that would connect the Atlantic to the Pacific. In 1903, the U.S. bought a strip of land at the Isthmus of Panama so a canal could be built. The first ship passed through the Panama Canal on August 15, 1914.

The growing involvement of the United States in world affairs affected North Carolina. The Spanish-American War took attention away from reforms. Expansion and the Panama Canal opened new markets for many products.

4. **DRAW YOUR ANSWER** Draw a simple diagram that shows the purpose of the Panama Canal.

LOOk Cl⊕ser

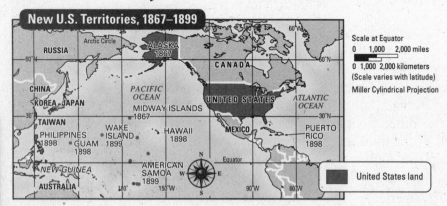

New U.S. Territories, 1867–1899

Scale at Equator
0 1,000 2,000 miles
0 1,000 2,000 kilometers
(Scale varies with latitude)
Miller Cylindrical Projection

United States land

🖉 Mark It Up!

5. This map shows territories gained by the United States between 1867 and 1899.
   • **Draw** an arrow to the largest territory gained during these years.
   • **Circle** the four islands that became U.S. lands in 1898.
   • Where were most of the new island territories located?

_____

CHAPTER 19

SECTION 2

World War I and Its Impact on North Carolina
For use with pages 433–437

Before, You Learned
By the early 1900s, the United States was one of the richest nations in the world.

Now You Will Learn
Competition among industrial nations led to many small wars and then to World War I.

Preview Terms & Names

- **Central Powers:** World War I alliance of Germany, Austria-Hungary, the Ottoman Empire, and Bulgaria
- **Allied Powers:** World War I alliance of nations that fought the Central Powers
- **neutrality:** not choosing a side in a conflict
- **communism:** a system in which the government owns all property

Take Notes as You Read

1.

MAKING GENERALIZATIONS

Event: The war began in 1914 just after a young student killed the future leader of Austria-Hungary.

↓

Generalization:

Fact: Germany sent a telegram to Mexico urging the nation to declare war on the United States.

↓

Generalization:

The start of the war; An uneasy neutrality

On June 28, 1914, a 19-year-old Serbian student shot and killed Archduke Franz Ferdinand, the heir to the throne of Austria-Hungary. The assassin wanted Serbia to become a Serbian homeland.

The Austrian emperor declared war on Serbia, and sides were drawn quickly. The Central Powers included Austria-Hungary, Germany, and the Ottoman Empire. The Allied Powers included Serbia, France, Great Britain, Russia, Japan, and Italy. When the war began, the U.S. declared neutrality; it would not help either side. Most Americans, however, rooted for the Allies.

The United States declares war

Germany attacked boats carrying British and American passengers. Then, the German foreign minister sent a telegram to Mexico urging it to declare war on the United States. On April 6, 1917, Congress declared war on Germany.

2. Explain why Americans were not interested in the war when it began.

_____

_____

_____

CHAPTER 19

Name _____ Date _____

New inventions; The turning point of the war

Countries used the advances of the Industrial Revolution to make deadly weapons. Machine guns, poison gas, and tanks made the war brutal. Finally, a series of events in 1918 ended the war. In February, the Russian people revolted against their tsar, or emperor. The new government made peace with Germany. By June, the U.S. was sending 250,000 troops a month to France. In November, the German kaiser gave up his throne, and the Germans signed an agreement to end the war.

Making peace

In 1919, representatives from 32 nations met to write a peace agreement. The treaty blamed the war on Germany. Germany had to give up its colonies and pay for the war.

3. How did U.S. involvement change the war?

_____

_____

Changes in Russia

In 1920, a radical group took control of Russia and renamed the country the Soviet Union. They set up a government based on communism, a system in which the people have most of the power. However, only Communist Party members had power.

Effects of the war on North Carolina

The war brought changes to North Carolina. Over 86,000 North Carolinians, black and white, joined the armed forces. Many ordinary citizens worked in war-related industries or in the Red Cross. Those who had served overseas came home with a new outlook on the world.

4. DRAW YOUR ANSWER Draw a picture that shows one way that the war affected the people of North Carolina.

LOOk Cl⊕ser

Allied and Central Powers in Europe, World War I

Mark It Up!

5. This map shows which nations formed the Allied Powers and the Central Powers. It also shows which nations remained neutral.
   • **Circle** the names of the four nations that formed the Central Powers.

   • **Underline** the names of the nations that formed the Allied Powers.
   • **Write** the letter *N* on the nations that remained neutral.

CHAPTER 19

SECTION
3

The Roaring Twenties
For use with pages 440–443

Before, You Learned
Competition among industrial nations led to many small wars and then to World War I.

Now You Will Learn
After World War I, the Roaring Twenties brought good times and great changes.

Preview Terms & Names

- **civil rights:** rights guaranteed to citizens by the Constitution
- **discrimination:** treating people differently because of their race, beliefs, or heritage
- **consumer goods:** products made for use by the average person
- **credit:** a way of paying for something in small amounts until it is paid for in full

Take Notes as You Read

1.

MAKING GENERALIZATIONS

Fact: During the Red Scare, some Americans accused people they disliked of being Communists.

Event: In 1920, the Nineteenth Amendment gave women the right to vote.

Generalization:

Generalization:

The fear of Communists; Setting immigration limits

Some Americans feared that the United States would be taken over by Communists. This led to the Red Scare of the early 1920s. During this time, some groups of Americans began accusing citizens they disliked of being Communists. The Red Scare ended when citizens realized that Communists did not pose a threat.

Some Americans feared that immigrants would spread communism or take jobs away from American workers. In 1921, Congress passed a law to limit immigration. Immigrants from some countries were barred and immigration slowed to a trickle.

Citizenship for Native Americans; Civil rights for African Americans

Thousands of Native Americans had fought in the war. After the war, they believed they deserved full citizenship and civil rights. In 1924, they gained the right to vote.

Many African Americans fought in Europe or worked in factories during the war. The NAACP used the courts to help them gain civil rights.

2. Explain one challenge that both Native Americans and African Americans faced.

_____

_____

CHAPTER 19

Voting rights for women

In 1920, after years of work in the woman suffrage movement, the Nineteenth Amendment to the Constitution gave voting rights to women across the country.

The beginning of the consumer age

During the Roaring Twenties, businesses and industries boomed, providing jobs and good wages for workers. People around the country wanted to buy consumer goods, products made for use by the average person.

The automobile industry was especially successful during this time. States began paving roads and highways, and repair shops and gas stations were built. Cars brought jobs to over four million people.

3. DRAW YOUR ANSWER Draw a picture of a consumer good produced in the 1920s.

Buy now, pay later

In the 1920s, many Americans bought consumer goods on credit, a way of paying for something in small amounts until it is paid in full. This included an extra charge called interest. Many people spent more than they earned. This led to problems.

The Roaring Twenties in North Carolina

The 1920s changed the habits and attitudes of North Carolinians. Women began to cut their hair, wear shorter skirts, drive cars, and smoke. Bootleggers made illegal alcohol that was sold in "speakeasies." Cars became common, giving people more freedom.

4. How did women's lives change in North Carolina during the Roaring Twenties?

_____

_____

_____

Look Closer

Mark It Up!

5. This magazine cover shows a "flapper," a young woman who felt free to try new styles during the Roaring Twenties.
- **Circle** a part of the woman's appearance that shows a style that was new during the Roaring Twenties.
- **Write** three words that describe the people in the picture.

_____

_____

CHAPTER 19

SECTION
1
From Boom to Bust
For use with pages 449–453

Before, You Learned
After World War I, the roaring Twenties brought good times and great changes.

Now You Will Learn
The successful economy of the 1920s came to an end in 1929, as the nation entered its worst economic depression.

Preview Terms & Names

- **buying on margin:** way of purchasing stocks on credit
- **Black Tuesday:** October 29, 1929, the day the stock market collapsed
- **Great Depression:** economic depression that followed the 1929 stock market crash
- **O. Max Gardner:** North Carolina's governor during the Great Depression

Take Notes as You Read

1.

MAKING INFERENCES

Fact: By 1929, many people had purchased stocks by buying on margin.

Fact: Governor Gardner encouraged farmers to begin growing their own food during the Great Depression.

Inference: Most people thought stock prices would continue to increase dramatically.

Inference:

A rosy outlook; Weaknesses in the economy

As the U.S. economy grew during the Roaring Twenties, most Americans believed that life could only get better. President Herbert Hoover told them that poverty would soon disappear from the nation.

People had good reason to be optimistic. After World War I, industries became more efficient and produced more goods than ever. American consumers bought in record numbers. However, there were problems in the economy. Many families were poor and could only afford to buy goods on credit.

The Great Bull Market

Many people purchased stocks by buying on margin—paying a small part of the stock's price and borrowing the rest. If the stock rose in value, people could pay off their loans and make money. If the stock lost value, people lost money. By 1929, borrowers had reached their debt limits. Farmers and others could not afford to buy goods. The weaknesses in the economy had become clear.

2. Explain why many Americans bought goods on credit in the 1920s.

_____

_____

CHAPTER 20

The Crash of 1929

A series of events led to the Crash of 1929. People bought fewer goods, and manufacturers' profits dropped. People bought fewer stocks. Stock values fell, and people sold their stocks to pay their debts.

On October 29, known as Black Tuesday, the stock market collapsed. This Crash of 1929 started a terrible economic depression.

The Great Depression

By 1933, about 9,000 banks were forced to close, and many people lost their life savings. People stopped buying goods, and businesses went bankrupt. In 1933, 25 percent of the population was unemployed. Millions went hungry. This period became known as the Great Depression.

3. **DRAW YOUR ANSWER** Draw a symbol showing the stock market on Black Tuesday.

President Hoover responds

President Hoover tried to help by creating new work projects. He believed that people needed jobs rather than handouts of money. However, the Depression grew worse, and many people blamed Hoover.

The Depression in North Carolina

During the Depression, people in North Carolina lost their homes and businesses. The state's furniture and textile industries were hit hard.

Governor O. Max Gardner helped North Carolina survive. Like Hoover, Gardner believed that people needed jobs, not handouts. He also introduced the Live at Home Program, which encouraged farmers to begin raising food for their families.

4. Explain one way that President Hoover and Governor Gardner were alike.

_____

_____

LOOk Cl🔎ser

🖉 Mark It Up!

5. This newspaper reports the panic that occurred on Black Thursday, as stock owners rushed to sell their shares.
   - **Circle** the date of Black Thursday.
   - **Underline** the city where this newspaper was printed.

- Why do you think this day became known as "Black Thursday"?

_____

_____

SECTION 2
The New Deal and Its Impact on North Carolina
For use with pages 454–459

Before, You Learned
The successful economy of the 1920s came to an end in 1929, as the nation entered the Great Depression.

Now You Will Learn
The United States and North Carolina faced and eventually overcame severe economic challenges.

Preview Terms & Names

- **Franklin Delano Roosevelt:** elected president in 1932
- **New Deal:** Roosevelt's programs intended to end the Great Depression
- **fireside chats:** Roosevelt's radio addresses
- **Hundred Days:** first days of 1933 session of Congress
- **Social Security Act:** created a retirement fund for American workers

Take Notes as You Read

1.

MAKING INFERENCES	
Event: In the summer of 1932, veterans asked the government for their promised bonus money.	**Event:** In 1932, Roosevelt won the presidential election in a landslide.
Inference:	**Inference:**

Reaction to the Bonus Army; Roosevelt takes charge

In the summer of 1932, nearly 20,000 World War I veterans came to Washington, D.C., to request the bonus money they had been promised for their service. They became known as the Bonus Army. Hoover refused to pay the Bonus Army, and the U.S. Army used force to drive the veterans away. Many Americans blamed Hoover for this action.

Americans found new hope in Franklin Delano Roosevelt, or FDR, who was elected president in 1932. Roosevelt promised the people a set of solutions to their problems, known as the New Deal.

Roosevelt's New Deal; The Hundred Days

FDR used friendly radio addresses, called fireside chats, to explain aspects of the New Deal. He was also willing to try new ideas and change the way government worked. In a special session, Congress passed 15 bills to solve problems of the Depression, called the "three Rs": **relief** for the hungry and jobless; **recovery** for agriculture and industry; **reforms** to prevent another depression.

2. In your own words, explain FDR's main goals for Congress during the Hundred Days.

_____

_____

Responses to the New Deal

Some government leaders thought that the New Deal went too far. Others thought it did not go far enough. Even so, voters supported FDR in 1934 by electing more Democrats to Congress.

The Social Security Act becomes law; The New Deal in North Carolina

In August 1935, FDR got Congress to pass the Social Security Act. Under the act, workers paid into a fund that would give them money when they retired. The act also helped people in need.

FDR won all but two states in the 1936 election. He received overwhelming support from North Carolina.

3. Explain the purpose of the Social Security Act.

_____

_____

New Deal programs

The NRA (National Recovery Administration) regulated working conditions, hours, and wages. The AAA (Agricultural Adjustment Act) helped farmers by raising the prices of cotton and tobacco.

Many leaders in North Carolina were unhappy with this governmental interference. They resisted taking part in most relief programs.

The CCC was the most successful New Deal program in North Carolina. It hired young men to work on state projects, such as building hiking trails and parks. Yet North Carolina still suffered from the Depression throughout the 1930s.

4. **DRAW YOUR ANSWER** Draw a picture that shows the work done by the CCC.

LOOk Cl⊕ser

Roosevelt's New Deal			
Program	Initials	Dates	Goal
Civilian Conservation Corps	CCC	1933–1942	Controlled erosion; employed young men to plant trees, set up parks, build bridges
Tennessee Valley Authority	TVA	1933–	Built dams to provide electricity for seven Southern states
Federal Emergency Relief Administration	FERA	1933–1938	Offered direct relief to jobless workers
Agricultural Adjustment Administration	AAA	1933–1936	Paid farmers not to plant crops so that prices would rise
National Recovery Administration	NRA	1933–1935	Oversaw labor codes that protected wages, prices, and working conditions
Public Works Administration	PWA	1933–1939	Provided jobs through construction of courthouses, sewage plants, bridges, hospitals, and public housing
Federal Deposit Insurance Corporation	FDIC	1933–	Protected savings accounts in all federally approved banks
Securities and Exchange Commission	SEC	1934–	Regulated the stock exchange
Federal Housing Administration	FHA	1934–	Insured loans for mortgages
Rural Electrification Administration	REA	1935–	Offered loans to bring electricity to rural farming communities, including some in North Carolina
National Labor Relations Board	NLRB	1935–	Regulated and protected unions and investigated unfair labor practices
Works Progress Administration	WPA	1935–1942	Provided work for jobless writers, artists, and musicians; extended jobs to men and women through construction of hospitals, schools, and airports
Social Security Act	SSA	1935–	Set up pensions and unemployment insurance for workers; provided aid to the disabled

🖊 Mark It Up!

5. This table shows the New Deal programs.
   - **Underline** the goal of the Federal Housing Administration.

   - **Circle** the two programs that shared the goal of bringing electricity to the South.

Copyright © by McDougal Littell, a division of Houghton Mifflin Company

SECTION 1

Steps to War

For use with pages 467–470

Before, You Learned

The United States and North Carolina faced and eventually overcame the Depression.

Now You Will Learn

In the late 1930s, the rise of totalitarianism in Europe laid the groundwork for a second world war.

Preview Terms & Names

- **isolationism:** staying out of other nations' affairs
- **Benito Mussolini:** Fascist dictator of Italy
- **fascism:** a political system in which the state controls every aspect of people's lives
- **Adolf Hitler:** Nazi dictator of Germany
- **anti-Semitism:** discrimination against Jews
- **appeasement:** giving in to aggressors to prevent conflict

Take Notes as You Read

1.

SEQUENCING EVENTS		
1933	**1936**	**1939**
Adolf Hitler and the Nazi Party start a dictatorship in Germany. →	→	

American isolationism; Mussolini takes control of Italy; Hitler rises to power

Most Americans supported isolationism. Congress passed the Neutrality Acts, which made it illegal to make loans or sell weapons to nations at war. However, the United States was already too connected to the rest of the world to stay isolated.

In the 1920s and 1930s, both Italy and Germany were ruled by totalitarian dictators. In 1925, Benito Mussolini became dictator of Italy. His political party was called the Italian Fascist Party. In fascism, the state controls every part of people's lives. Mussolini and his followers used violence against anyone who opposed them.

In 1933, Germany became a dictatorship led by Adolf Hitler. Hitler was a member of the Nazi Party. Like the fascists, the Nazis took total control and crushed their enemies.

Hitler believed that the German, or Aryan, race was superior to all others. He argued that Germany had lost World War I because ordinary workers had been betrayed by the Jews. The Nazis began an official campaign of anti-Semitism.

2. In your own words, explain how the fascists and the Nazis were alike.

_____

_____

CHAPTER 21

Communist totalitarianism in the Soviet Union; The military takes control in Japan

In the Soviet Union, Josef Stalin became dictator in 1924. He forced all farmers to work together on large farms. Millions of farmers were killed, and the Soviet people suffered from widespread famine.

Around the same time, a dictatorship was coming to power in Japan. In 1931, Japan attacked Manchuria, China. Japan then put the military in charge of its government.

Totalitarianism leads to aggression

Fascists, Nazis, and militarists all believed that strong nations had to conquer other nations to survive. In 1936, Hitler and Mussolini signed an alliance called the Rome-Berlin Axis.

3. **DRAW YOUR ANSWER** Draw a symbol that represents the Rome-Berlin Axis.

Appeasement at Munich; Germany starts the war

In 1938, Hitler took control of Austria. Next, he demanded control of the Sudetenland, part of Czechoslovakia. Britain and France allowed Hitler to take the land as long as he promised to take no more territory.

In the spring of 1939, Hitler conquered the rest of Czechoslovakia. In August, he signed a Non-Aggression Pact with the Soviet Union. In the pact, the countries agreed to not fight each other and to split Poland between them.

Britain and France warned Hitler that invading Poland would start a war. Nevertheless, Hitler sent troops into Poland on September 1, 1939. Two days later, Britain and France declared war.

4. Explain why appeasement failed to stop Hitler's plans for conquest.

_____

_____

LOOk Closer

PRIMARY SOURCE

The Fascist State is itself conscious. . . . The State is a spiritual and moral fact in itself . . . a manifestation [outward form] of the spirit. . . . Everything within the state, nothing outside the state, nothing against the state . . . the state [is] an absolute.

Benito Mussolini

Mark It Up!

5. In this quotation, Benito Mussolini explains his beliefs about government.
   • **Circle** the political party Mussolini mentions in the quotation.
   • **Underline** three words or phrases Mussolini uses to describe "the State."

SECTION
2

War in Europe and Africa

For use with pages 471–477

Before, You Learned

The rise of totalitarianism laid the groundwork for a second world war.

Now You Will Learn

The United States entered World War II on the side of the Allies, who defeated the Axis powers in Europe in 1945.

Preview Terms & Names

- **blitzkrieg:** Germany's "lightning war" tactics
- **Tripartite Alliance:** wartime alliance between Germany, Italy, and Japan
- **D-Day:** Allied invasion that freed France
- **Holocaust:** German killing of Jews
- **concentration camps:** prison camps where millions of Jews were murdered

CHAPTER 21

Take Notes as You Read

1.

SEQUENCING EVENTS		
December 7, 1941	**September 1943**	**May 7, 1945** German forces surrender, ending the war in Europe.

The fall of Europe; The United States moves away from isolationism

Germany destroyed Poland in a matter of weeks. Germany's war tactics were so rapid and deadly that they were known as blitzkrieg, or "lightning war." In April 1940, Hitler used blitzkrieg to conquer most of Europe. Britain was the only country that successfully defended itself.

President Roosevelt became convinced that the United States had to help the Allies. In 1941, he pushed Congress to pass the Lend-Lease Act, which allowed the U.S. to lend or lease equipment and weapons to the Allied nations. The U.S. sent about $50 billion worth of war goods to the Allies.

The Tripartite Alliance; Pearl Harbor

In 1940, Japan joined the Axis powers in the Tripartite Alliance. In response, the U.S. stopped all trade with Japan. Japan decided to destroy the U.S. Navy's Pacific fleet. On December 7, 1941, Japanese warplanes bombed the American naval base at Pearl Harbor. Over 2,400 Americans died. The next day, Congress declared war on Japan. On December 11, Hitler and Mussolini declared war on the United States.

2. **DRAW YOUR ANSWER** Draw a diagram that represents the Tripartite Alliance.

Germany attacks the Soviet Union

On June 22, 1941, Germany invaded Russia but failed to conquer key Soviet cities. With help from the Allies, Soviet forces finally defeated the Germans.

Battles in Africa and Italy

In 1942, Allied troops won several key battles in North Africa. Then in 1943, the Allies invaded Italy. In September, Mussolini was arrested and Italy surrendered. However, Germany was in charge of Italy.

The Allied advance and D-Day

On June 6, 1944, more than 130,000 American, British, and Canadian soldiers landed on the coast of Normandy, France, in the D-Day invasion. By the end of the day, Allied forces had taken control of the beaches. Allied forces moved through France, and by February 1945, German troops were retreating everywhere.

Victory in Europe

In April 1945, President Roosevelt died, and Harry S. Truman became president. He continued the war effort. German forces surrendered on May 7. The Allies declared May 8 Victory in Europe Day.

The horrors of the Holocaust

In Germany, Allied soldiers found prison camps, known as concentration camps, where millions of Jews and others had been murdered. In 1941, Hitler had called for all Jews to be killed. This genocide is known as the Holocaust.

After the war, the Allies set up special courts where Nazi leaders and others were tried for the crimes of the Holocaust. These trials were called the Nuremberg Trials.

4. Explain why May 8 is known as V-E Day.

_____

_____

_____

LOOk Closer

Copyright © by McDougal Littell, a division of Houghton Mifflin Company

PRIMARY SOURCE

We shall fight on the beaches, we shall fight on the landing grounds, we shall fight in the fields, and in the streets, we shall fight in the hills; we shall never surrender.

British Prime Minister Winston Churchill

Mark It Up!

5. In this quotation, Winston Churchill discusses the war against Germany.
- **Circle** the five locations where Churchill promises the British will fight.
- **Underline** the one thing Churchill states that the British will **not** do.

SECTION 3
War in the Pacific
For use with pages 478–481

Before, You Learned
The United States entered World War II on the side of the Allies.

Now You Will Learn
The United States developed new war strategies and atomic weapons, helping to defeat the Japanese and end the war.

Preview Terms & Names

- **Douglas MacArthur:** general who led troops to regain the Philippines in March 1945
- **Bataan Death March:** a forced march in which 10,000 Allied troops died
- **island hopping:** Allies' plan for the war in the Pacific
- **Manhattan Project:** a top-secret U.S. project to develop an atomic bomb

Take Notes as You Read

1.

SEQUENCING EVENTS		
June 1942	**August 1945**	
The Allies won a key victory over the Japanese in the Pacific at the Battle of Midway. →	→	

The Philippines
By the spring of 1942, Japan had attacked many territories held by the Allies in the Pacific. Japan also attacked the Philippines. American and Filipino troops led by General Douglas MacArthur withdrew to the Bataan Peninsula.

When MacArthur was sent to defend Australia, Japanese forces attacked the troops that remained. The Japanese captured 70,000 soldiers and forced them to march 60 miles to a prison camp. About 10,000 soldiers died on the march, known as the Bataan Death March.

The Allies turn the tide at Midway
The Allies began to gain ground against the Japanese in 1942. In April, Lieutenant Colonel James Doolittle led an air raid against Japanese cities. The raid did little damage but boosted the Allies' morale. In May, the U.S. Navy blocked a Japanese attack against Australia in the Battle of the Coral Sea. In June, the U.S. Navy defeated a Japanese fleet at the Battle of Midway. This victory allowed the Allies to go on the attack.

2. Why was the Battle of Midway important?

_____

_____

CHAPTER 21

CHAPTER 21

The Allies advance

The Allies used a strategy known as island hopping to regain control of the Pacific. They conquered small islands, and then used the islands as bases. By October 1944, they had reached the Philippines. MacArthur and his troops regained the Philippines in March 1945.

Iwo Jima and Okinawa

By early 1945, the Allies began bombing Japan. That spring, they invaded two small Japanese islands, Iwo Jima and Okinawa, which they planned to use as bases. The Japanese fiercely defended both islands, but the Allies eventually succeeded.

3. DRAW YOUR ANSWER Draw a picture that shows the strategy of island hopping.

Atomic weapons end the war

By the summer of 1945, the United States had developed a powerful new weapon, the atomic bomb. The bomb was created by scientists who worked on the top-secret Manhattan Project. Using the bomb would save American lives that would be lost if the U.S. invaded Japan.

On August 6, 1945, the U.S. dropped an atomic bomb on the city of Hiroshima. Over 70,000 people were killed. When the Japanese refused to surrender, the U.S. dropped a second bomb on Nagasaki. Japan finally surrendered. World War II officially ended on September 2, 1945.

4. In your own words, explain why the U.S. decided to drop atomic bombs on Japan.

_____

_____

_____

LOOk Closer

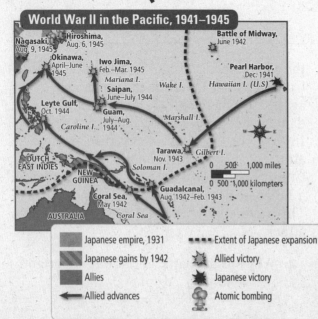

World War II in the Pacific, 1941–1945

Nagasaki, Aug. 9, 1945
Hiroshima, Aug. 6, 1945
Okinawa, April–June 1945
Iwo Jima, Feb.–Mar. 1945
Mariana I.
Saipan, June–July 1944
Leyte Gulf, Oct. 1944
Guam, July–Aug. 1944
Caroline I.
Wake I.
Marshall I.
Battle of Midway, June 1942
Pearl Harbor, Dec. 1941
Hawaiian I. (U.S)
DUTCH EAST INDIES
NEW GUINEA
Tarawa, Nov. 1943
Soloman I.
Gilbert I.
Coral Sea, May 1942
Guadalcanal, Aug. 1942–Feb. 1943
AUSTRALIA
Coral Sea
0   500   1,000 miles
0 500 1,000 kilometers

Japanese empire, 1931
Japanese gains by 1942
Allies
Allied advances
Extent of Japanese expansion
Allied victory
Japanese victory
Atomic bombing

Mark It Up!

5. This map shows battles that took place in the Pacific during World War II. It also shows Allied and Japanese territories.
- **Circle** the two locations where the Allies dropped atomic bombs.
- **Draw** an arrow to the location of the Battle of Midway.
- **Write** the letter *J* at the site of a battle won by the Japanese, and write the letter *A* at the site of a battle won by the Allies.

Copyright © by McDougal Littell, a division of Houghton Mifflin Company

SECTION
4

Impact of the War on North Carolina

For use with pages 482–487

Before, You Learned
The United States developed new war strategies and atomic weapons, helping to defeat the Japanese and end the war.

Now You Will Learn
The commitment to winning the war changed the way North Carolinians lived and worked.

Preview Terms & Names

- **rationing:** system of limiting goods
- **internment camps:** camps where Japanese Americans were held during the war
- **Torpedo Junction:** war-time nickname for the waters off Cape Hatteras
- **Margaret O. Craighill:** the first woman to serve as an army doctor

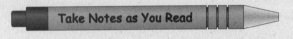
Take Notes as You Read

1.

SEQUENCING EVENTS		
1941	**1942–1945**	**1945**
→	→	Women made up 30 percent of the American workforce.

Wartime production; The workforce; Wartime restrictions

Under the guidance of the War Production Board, American factories made huge amounts of war materials such as planes, tanks, and weapons. Jobs became easy to find. Women workers, too, were in demand. By 1945, women made up about 30 percent of the workforce. The war also provided jobs for many African Americans and Hispanic Americans. Many people left the South to move to Northern cities where most of the new jobs were located.

Items such as gasoline, meat, and shoes became scarce. To divide these goods fairly, the government used rationing, a system in which families were allowed to have only fixed amounts of certain items every month.

The internment of Japanese Americans

After the attack on Pearl Harbor, Japanese Americans fell under suspicion. In 1942, President Roosevelt had Japanese and Japanese Americans living on the West Coast put in internment camps. Fears about the Japanese Americans were unfounded.

2. Explain how the U.S. workforce changed during the war.

_____

_____

The war in North Carolina; Tar Heels in the armed forces

North Carolina was involved in the war from the start. The waters off Cape Hatteras became known as Torpedo Junction because of German submarine attacks there. Hospitals set up special burn units to take care of badly injured sailors.

More than 350,000 North Carolinians served in the war. Women worked in support services or as nurses. Dr. Margaret O. Craighill, of Southport, was the first female army doctor.

3. **DRAW YOUR ANSWER** Draw a picture that shows a role that women served in the war.

North Carolina's training bases and war industries; The war's impact

North Carolina provided major military training facilities. Many new bases were opened. By the end of the war, more soldiers had been trained in North Carolina than in any other state. North Carolina's war industries produced ships, parachutes, and ammunition. Farmers grew wheat, peanuts, and potatoes. Workers were in demand.

North Carolina made a number of reforms during the war. In 1944, the state instituted a full nine-month school year and added the twelfth grade. The Assembly provided equal salaries for black and white teachers. The state's economy had grown much stronger. Men and women returned from overseas with a more tolerant view of the world.

4. Explain how North Carolina improved education during the war.

_____

_____

_____

LOOk Closer

World War II Military Installations in North Carolina

1	Camp Battle, New Bern	14	Naval Air Station, Elizabeth City
2	Bluethenthal Field, Wilmington	15	Pope Field, Fort Bragg
3	Fort Bragg near Fayetteville	16	Raleigh-Durham Army Field, Raleigh
4	Camp Butner near Durham	17	Camp Sutton, Monroe
5	Cherry Point Marine Air Station, Havelock	18	Fort Macon, Morehead City
6	Coast Guard Station, Elizabeth City	19	Charlotte Quartmaster Depot, Charlotte
7	Camp Davis, Holly Ridge	20	Winston-Salem Municipal Airport, Winston-Salem
8	Seymour-Johnson Field, Goldsboro	21	Army Air Force Replacement Center, Greensboro
9	Knollwood Field near Aberdeen	22	Army Air Force Redistribution Rest Camp, Lake Lure
10	Laurinburg-Maxton Air Base, Maxton		
11	Camp Lejeune, Jacksonville		
12	Camp Mackall, Hoffman		
13	Morris Field, Charlotte		

✐ Mark It Up!

5. This map shows military installations in North Carolina during World War II.

• **Circle** the numbers of the 8 installations located on North Carolina's coast.

• **Underline** the name of the installation closest to the Appalachian Mountains.

• Which region of North Carolina had the *fewest* military installations at the time?

_____

SECTION 1

Changes in Society

For use with pages 495–497

Before, You Learned
The United States played a key role in helping the Allies win World War II.

Now You Will Learn
The war's end brought changes to the way Americans, including North Carolinians, lived and worked.

Preview Terms & Names

- **suburb:** residential area on the outskirts of a city
- **refugee:** person fleeing a home country to avoid being persecuted or killed

Take Notes as You Read

1.

Significant Changes in the U.S. and North Carolina	
Workforce	**Lifestyle**
• New industries brought new kinds of jobs.	•
•	•

New industries

By the end of World War II, the United States had become the world's leading industrial nation. From the early 1900s, fewer people worked in agriculture or small businesses, and more worked for large companies. After 1945, people switched from producing goods to working in the service industry as doctors, nurses, repair persons, and computer programmers.

Women in the workforce

During the war, millions of women filled the jobs that had been left behind by men called off to battle. Many women continued to work after the war because they needed the

income or liked the independence their jobs brought.

By the 1980s, over half of the women in America worked outside the home. Many held low-paying jobs, but some women entered jobs in fields like law and medicine, and a few pioneers became construction workers, airplane pilots, or police officers. Women also began to hold offices in state and national government.

2. When did many women first enter the American workforce?

_____

_____

CHAPTER 22

A nation of consumers

After World War II:

- Factories switched from making war supplies to consumer goods.
- Americans, including women and children, had more money to spend.
- People bought goods that made their lives easier and more fun.

World markets and competition

For decades after the war, the United States sold the most manufactured goods and agricultural products. As other nations rebuilt their factories, they offered goods that cost less. The United States began importing more goods than it exported.

3. DRAW YOUR ANSWER Draw a scene that shows Americans shopping for goods.

Towns and suburbs grow; Changing population

Industry grew and transportation improved. This caused the growth of

- smaller towns like Chapel Hill.
- suburbs, which are residential areas on the outskirts of cities.

After the war ended, many couples started families, causing a baby boom. As thousands of immigrants also arrived, the population grew even larger.

During the 1960s, Congress passed a new immigration law that ended the favoring of certain countries. It also made immigration easier for refugees, people who flee their own countries out of fear of being treated badly or even killed because of their political beliefs.

4. In your own words, give *two* reasons for population growth after World War II.

_____

_____

_____

LOOk Clㅇser

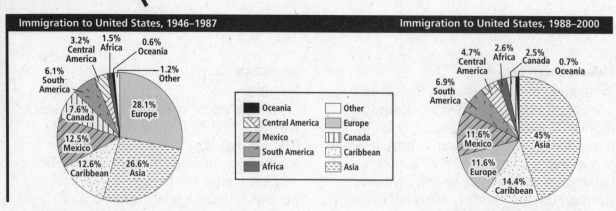

Immigration to United States, 1946–1987

3.2% Central America
1.5% Africa
0.6% Oceania
1.2% Other
6.1% South America
28.1% Europe
7.6% Canada
12.5% Mexico
12.6% Caribbean
26.6% Asia

Oceania
Central America
Mexico
South America
Africa
Other
Europe
Canada
Caribbean
Asia

Immigration to United States, 1988–2000

4.7% Central America
2.6% Africa
2.5% Canada
0.7% Oceania
6.9% South America
11.6% Mexico
45% Asia
11.6% Europe
14.4% Caribbean

✎ Mark It Up!

5. This chart shows the percentages of U.S. immigrants from different areas during two time periods.

- **Circle** the place where most immigrants came from until 1987.

- **Underline** the place where most immigrants came from after 1988.
- **Which** area had the most growth in U.S. immigration over time?

CHAPTER 22

SECTION 2

Economic and Technological Changes

For use with pages 498–502

Before, You Learned
Americans lived and worked in new places after World War II.

Now You Will Learn
With economic success from research and industry, North Carolina has great opportunity, yet also faces challenges.

Preview Terms & Names

- **Research Triangle Park:** national research institute created in North Carolina in 1961
- **Environmental Management Commission:** agency that protects North Carolina's natural resources
- **acid rain:** rainfall that carries harmful chemicals
- **erosion:** the wearing away of soil and sand by wind or water

Take Notes as You Read

1.

Significant Changes in North Carolina	
Industry	**Improvements to Everyday Life**
• The state's primary industries—textiles, tobacco, and furniture—continued to grow.	•
•	•

The Research Triangle Park is created
After World War II, North Carolina worked to build its research and scientific industry. In 1961, the Research Triangle Park was created. This national research institute brought together people from private businesses and government agencies all over the world. They developed new solutions to worldwide problems.

New efforts lead to new advances
North Carolina moved forward in other areas. It was the first state to require that all children receive a vaccine for the disease of polio. Widespread distribution followed, and the disease was mostly wiped out.

North Carolina also created the "Go Forward" program. Through "Go Forward," school construction and state agencies received more funding. Thousands of miles of paved roads were built. Power and telephone lines were run farther into the countryside for the people who lived and worked there.

2. In your own words, explain why North Carolina created Research Triangle Park.

_____

_____

CHAPTER 22

CHAPTER 22 SECTION 2: ECONOMIC AND TECHNOLOGICAL CHANGES, *CONTINUED*

Economic changes spur improvements in higher education

North Carolina's economy changed during the 1950s and 1960s.

- New industries like computer manufacturing and banking services grew.
- Residents needed to learn skills in order to work in the new industries.
- Colleges and training centers were built.
- State funds were set aside for public education and new programs.

The arts benefit

North Carolina's new businesses were successful; the state earned more tax money. Some of this money funded arts programs and built new art and history museums.

3. Why did more North Carolinians seek higher education in the 1950s and 1960s?

_____

_____

North Carolinians respond to threats to the environment

In 1973, North Carolina created the Environmental Management Commission. This agency protected the state's natural resources and worked to reduce pollution and soil erosion. This work led to laws limiting air and water pollution. This helped prevent acid rain from killing many trees.

Environmental challenges remain

North Carolina still faces the problem of erosion, the slow wearing away of soil and sand. Lawmakers and communities are working on the issue. The state also faces the problem of disposing of nuclear and chemical waste from nuclear power plants.

4. **DRAW YOUR ANSWER** Draw a picture that shows one of North Carolina's environmental challenges.

LOOk Closer

PRIMARY SOURCE

To the east, in North Carolina, was the area known as the Research Triangle, bounded by the university campuses of Chapel Hill, Raleigh, and Durham, where over a period of almost thirty years a big industrial park of seventy-five hundred acres had been created: thirty thousand new jobs there, poor North Carolina pineland landscaped into the discreetest kind of industrial garden, many modern technological and pharmaceutical names represented by new buildings . . . giving an impression of spaciousness and order and elegance, the land of rural poverty remade to suit its new function.

V. S. Naipaul, *Turn in the South*

✎ Mark It Up!

5. **Read** the primary source quotation.
   - **Circle** three words that describe Naipaul's impression of the park.
   - **Underline** the names of three university campuses that border the park.
   - **Why** do you think the park was built near universities?

_____

_____

CHAPTER 22

SECTION 3

Changes in North Carolina's Government

For use with pages 503–505

Before, You Learned
North Carolina has great opportunity, yet also faces challenges.

Now You Will Learn
The state's government and constitution were updated to reflect changes in North Carolina.

Preview Terms & Names

- **North Carolina Fund:** a program created in 1963 to end the cycle of poverty in North Carolina
- **cooperative:** an organization run by members of the same profession or group, allowing them to share resources

Take Notes as You Read

1.

Changes in North Carolina's Government		
The state government reduced and reorganized its administrative departments.		

The state government is reorganized

- 1953: The Commission on the Reorganization of State Government was created. Its purpose was to study and improve North Carolina's government.
- 1967: The State Constitution Study Commission was formed. It recommended updates to North Carolina's constitution.
- November 3, 1970: The reorganization amendment was passed. It reduced the number of state administrative departments from 350 to 25.
- 1971–1973: The governor reorganized the remaining departments.

The state legislature gets a new facility

In 1963, the General Assembly funded the construction of a new building for North Carolina's legislature. The new building was the first in the country to be built only for use by a state legislature.

2. In your own words, explain the effects of the executive reorganization amendment.

_____

_____

CHAPTER 22

State government encourages economic development

The state government helped North Carolina's economy grow. Officials traveled far to convince businesses to come to the state, bringing the promise of many high-paying jobs.

The North Carolina Fund creates new opportunities

In 1963, the North Carolina Fund was created to help the poor. The programs included a farmers' cooperative, which allowed people to share resources. The fund improved schools, provided housing, and educated people about voting, health, and jobs.

3. **DRAW YOUR ANSWER** Draw a picture that represents the North Carolina Fund.

The Republican Party gains strength

North Carolina has traditionally been a Democratic state. It did not have a Republican governor from 1896 until 1972. After 1972, the Republican Party began to fill more government posts. This led to a more workable two-party system in North Carolina. Key events include:

- 1972: Republican James E. Holshouser, Jr. is elected governor.
- 1977: Democrat James B. Hunt, Jr., becomes governor.
- 1981: Governor Hunt becomes the first governor in modern times to serve two full terms.

4. In your own words, explain how North Carolina's government changed after 1972.

_____

_____

_____

LO🔍k Cl🔍ser

North Carolina Voting in Presidential Elections, 1944–1976

🖉 Mark It Up!

5. This graph shows the number of votes received by Democratic and Republican presidential candidates in North Carolina.
   - **Underline** the political party that received more votes in most elections from 1944 to 1976.
   - **Circle** the election year when North Carolina's voting pattern changed.

   - **Write** a sentence describing Republican voting patterns in North Carolina.

   _____

   _____

SECTION 1
Origins of the Civil Rights Movement
For use with pages 513–517

Before, You Learned
The United States and North Carolina underwent significant changes.

Now You Will Learn
African Americans began to succeed in their efforts to gain full political rights and to end segregation.

Preview Terms & Names

- **segregation:** the separation of races within society
- ***Brown*** v. ***Board of Education of Topeka:*** Supreme Court ruling that segregation in schools is unconstitutional
- **Rosa Parks:** woman whose arrest started the Montgomery bus boycott
- **Martin Luther King, Jr.:** leader of the civil rights movement

Take Notes as You Read

1.

ANALYZING CAUSES AND EFFECTS	
Causes:	**Effects:**
Linda Brown was not allowed to attend an all-white school in Topeka, Kansas	*Brown* v. *Board of Education of Topeka*
	Montgomery bus boycott

Postwar changes strengthen the civil rights movement; Challenging segregation

Postwar changes helped make the civil rights movement successful. More Americans began to see racism as evil, especially after the Holocaust. African Americans were more determined to win freedom after fighting for freedom in Europe during the war. Many African Americans worked in cities and formed contacts with one another. In the early 1950s, some African Americans sued to end segregation in public schools.

Brown v. Board of Education of Topeka

In 1951, school officials in Topeka, Kansas, refused to allow an African-American

girl, Linda Brown, to attend an all-white school. Her parents and the NAACP fought for her rights. The case, *Brown* v. *Board of Education of Topeka,* eventually went to the Supreme Court.

In 1954, the Supreme Court ruled that segregation in public schools was unconstitutional. Integration still did not happen easily. In some communities, federal troops had to protect students from mobs.

2. Explain the main effect of the *Brown* v. *Board of Education of Topeka* ruling.

_____

_____

CHAPTER 23

The Montgomery bus boycott; Massive resistance

In 1955, Rosa Parks was arrested after refusing to give up her seat on a bus to a white rider. News of her arrest spread; many people began to boycott the city's buses.

The Supreme Court ruled that the bus segregation law was unconstitutional. People were then allowed to sit where they chose, so the bus boycott ended. Dr. Martin Luther King, Jr., was a leader of the boycott. He became a leading figure in the civil rights movement.

Many Southern whites opposed desegregation. Opposition, known as massive resistance, slowed down desegregation in many Southern states. The Ku Klux Klan also used violence to threaten African Americans who tried to use their civil rights.

3. Explain the purpose of massive resistance.

_____

_____

Showdown in Little Rock

In 1957, the school board and governor of Little Rock, Arkansas, tried to prevent nine African-American students from enrolling in Central High School. For three weeks, the governor had National Guard troops block the students from the school. Finally, President Dwight Eisenhower sent federal troops to protect the students.

Sit-ins energize the movement

A number of protesters took part in sit-ins, protests in which people sit in a place and refuse to move until their demands are met. Many sit-ins took place at segregated lunch counters. Sit-ins forced many stores to desegregate their lunch counters.

4. **DRAW YOUR ANSWER** Draw a picture that shows protesters at a sit-in.

LOOk Closer

✏ Mark It Up!

5. In this photograph, a group of women protest against the integration of their children's elementary school.
   - **Underline** the message on the sign that has to do with segregation.
   - **Write** three words that describe the attitude of the women in this photograph.

_____

_____

_____

CHAPTER 23

SECTION
2

The Civil Rights Movement Expands
For use with pages 518–522

Before, You Learned
African Americans began to succeed in their efforts to end segregation.

Now You Will Learn
During the 1960s, the civil rights movement grew, and laws designed to protect people's basic rights were passed.

Preview Terms & Names

- **March on Washington:** 1963 demonstration for civil rights attended by 250,000 people
- **Civil Rights Act of 1964:** law that officially banned segregation in public places
- **Freedom Summer:** 1964 program to register black voters
- **Voting Rights Act:** banned laws that kept blacks from registering to vote

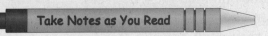
Take Notes as You Read

1.

ANALYZING CAUSES AND EFFECTS	
Events:	**Effects:**
Civil Rights Act of 1964	• • Prevented job discrimination
Equal Rights Amendment	• Not approved by enough states •

Protests in Birmingham

In 1963, African Americans in Birmingham, Alabama, began protesting to integrate public facilities and gain better job and housing opportunities. Dr. Martin Luther King, Jr., took part and was arrested. The police used dogs and fire hoses on the protesters.

People across the nation were horrified when they saw these events on television. Soon, Birmingham's white leaders agreed to end segregation in public places and employ more African Americans in downtown stores.

The events in Birmingham made many Americans favor new laws to protect the civil rights of all people.

The March on Washington; New laws

In 1963, about 250,000 people took part in the March on Washington, a civil rights demonstration. At this march, King gave his famous "I Have a Dream" speech.

President John F. Kennedy supported civil rights, but he was assassinated in 1963. The new president, Lyndon B. Johnson, signed the Civil Rights Act of 1964. It banned segregation in public places and helped prevent job discrimination.

2. Why was the March on Washington held?

_____

_____

CHAPTER 23

Fighting for rights

Even after the Civil Rights Act of 1964, many African Americans in the South still had problems voting. Volunteers went to Mississippi to help register black voters in a program called Freedom Summer. The volunteers registered 1,200 African American voters. On August 6, 1965, the Voting Rights Act became law. It banned laws that prevented African Americans from registering to vote.

Hispanic Americans and Native Americans also worked to achieve greater civil rights. In 1974, the Supreme Court ruled that schools must provide bilingual education for children who do not speak English. In the 1970s, the U.S. government was forced to pay for or return lands taken from Native Americans.

3. Explain one effect of the Voting Rights Act.

_____

_____

Women and the Equal Rights Amendment

By the 1960s, women still did not have the same opportunities as men. Congress passed the Equal Rights Amendment (ERA) in 1972, but not enough states approved it. Congress did pass laws guaranteeing equal job opportunities and pay.

Physically challenged Americans and older Americans

In the 1970s, Congress stated that people cannot be denied jobs just because they are physically challenged. They also ruled that public buildings must be accessible to all.

Older Americans formed groups to fight for their goals as well.

4. **DRAW YOUR ANSWER** Draw a symbol that represents the goal of the Equal Rights Amendment.

LOOk Closer

PRIMARY SOURCE

I guess it is easy for those who have never felt the stinging darts of segregation to say, "Wait.". . . [But] there comes a time when the cup of endurance runs over, and men are no longer willing to be plunged into an abyss [a bottomless pit] of injustice.

Martin Luther King, Jr., *"Letter from Birmingham Jail"*

Mark It Up!

5. In this letter, Martin Luther King, Jr., defends civil rights protests held in Birmingham, Alabama.
   - **Read** the primary source quotation.
   - **Circle** the two words that describe how segregation feels.
   - **Underline** the place to which Dr. King compares injustice.

CHAPTER 23

SECTION
3 | Civil Rights in North Carolina
For use with pages 523–527

Before, You Learned
The civil rights movement grew, leading to the passage of laws designed to protect people's basic rights.

Now You Will Learn
African Americans and women in North Carolina fought to gain equal rights.

Preview Terms & Names

- **Pearsall Plan:** a plan that, if passed, would have allowed schools in North Carolina to close by majority vote rather than integrate
- **busing:** transporting children to different school districts in order to integrate the schools

Take Notes as You Read

1.

ANALYZING CAUSES AND EFFECTS		
Causes:	Events:	Effects:
	The Supreme Court required Charlotte schools to use busing.	
Native Americans lacked full civil rights in North Carolina.	Native American groups were officially recognized.	

African Americans fight school segregation; The Pearsall Plan is adopted

In the 1950s, African Americans began to fight for the right to attend the same schools that other people of North Carolina attended.

In March 1951, a court ordered the University of North Carolina to admit African Americans. In 1955, the North Carolina General Assembly passed a resolution claiming integration would never work. The Pearsall Plan allowed schools to close by majority vote rather than integrate. It was not put into practice, and schools began to integrate. By 1960, few state schools had integrated, and in 1964, the Civil Rights Act stepped up integration.

Busing helps integrate schools

In 1969, the Charlotte school system was given a court order to integrate, even if it required busing students from one district to another. The case went to the Supreme Court, where the ruling was upheld. Busing became a powerful tool for integration in North Carolina as well as in other states.

2. DRAW YOUR ANSWER Draw a diagram that shows the process of busing students.

CHAPTER 23

Copyright © by McDougal Littell, a division of Houghton Mifflin Company

African Americans resist discrimination and enter state politics

African Americans resisted many unfair practices by holding protests called sit-ins. In 1960, African-American students held a sit-in at a segregated lunch counter in a Woolworth's store in Greensboro. The event, called the Greensboro "Coffee Party," sparked sit-ins across the country.

During the years of integration, African Americans took part in state government. Henry E. Frye was elected to the General Assembly in 1968 and to the North Carolina Supreme Court in 1983. Howard N. Lee was elected mayor of Chapel Hill in 1969.

3. In your own words, explain the purpose of the Greensboro "Coffee Party."

_____

_____

Women and Native Americans in North Carolina seek equal rights

Women in North Carolina made progress toward equality in the 1960s and 1970s. In 1962, Judge Susie Marshall Sharp became the first woman on the North Carolina Supreme Court. In 1968, Margaret Taylor Harper was the first woman to run for statewide office. In 1972, Isabelle Cannon became the first female mayor in North Carolina.

During the 1960s and 1970s, many Native American groups were recognized by the state government. This brought better opportunities and greater freedoms. The state also created the Commission of Indian Affairs to promote the rights of Native Americans.

4. Explain one civil rights gain made by Native Americans during the 1960s and 1970s.

_____

_____

LOOk Closer

There was a little old white lady who was finishing up her coffee at the counter. She strode toward me and I said to myself, 'Oh my, someone to spit in my face or slap my face.' I was prepared for it. But she stands behind Joseph McNeil and me and puts her hands on our shoulders. She said, "Boys, I'm so proud of you. I only regret that you didn't do this 10 years ago." That was probably the biggest boost, morally, that I got that whole day, and probably the biggest boost for me during the entire movement.

Franklin McCain, *"Voices of Civil Rights"*

Mark It Up!

5. In this quotation, Franklin McCain describes taking part in the Greensboro "Coffee Party."
   - **Read** the primary source quotation.
   - **Circle** what McCain thought would happen when the woman first approached him.
   - **Underline** the message the woman shared with McCain.

CHAPTER 23

SECTION
1

The Cold War Roots of the Conflict
For use with pages 533–537

Before, You Learned
African Americans and other groups worked to achieve greater rights during the 1950s, 1960s, and 1970s.

Now You Will Learn
After World War II, U.S. efforts to stop communism's spread included involvement in the Korean War.

Preview Terms & Names

- **Cold War:** rivalry between the United States and the Soviet Union and other Communist countries
- **containment:** U.S. policy of trying to stop the spread of communism
- **brinksmanship:** aggressive U.S. policy that called for the overthrow of Communist governments and going to the brink of war to combat communism

Take Notes as You Read

1.

CATEGORIZING		
Reasons for Involvement in the Korean War		
The United States	**The Soviet Union**	**South Korea**
•	• supported Communist North Korea against South Korea	•

The Cold War; Fear at home
During World War II, the United States and the Soviet Union worked together to defeat Nazi Germany. However, the Soviet Union took over European countries after freeing them from Nazi rule. The Soviets also refused to give up part of Germany. Germany was split: democratic in the west and Communist in the east.

U.S. President Truman used a strategy known as containment to stop the spread of communism. The U.S. and other democracies formed the North Atlantic Treaty Organization (NATO). In response, the Soviet Union and Eastern European nations formed the Warsaw Pact.

After World War II, many Americans feared the growth of communism at home. President Truman required government workers to swear loyalty to the United States. Senator Joseph McCarthy took the hunt for Communists to a controversial level. He accused hundreds of government officials of belonging to the Communist Party, but the charges were never proven. Even so, he ruined the careers of thousands of people.

2. In your own words, explain why Germany was split after World War II.

_____

_____

Name _____ Date _____

CHAPTER 24

The Korean War

When World War II ended in 1945, the Asian nation of Korea was split in two. North Korea, with the help of the Soviets, developed a Communist government. South Korea, aided by the United States, had a non-Communist leader.

Fighting breaks out

In June 1950, North Korea invaded South Korea, starting the Korean War. The United States and United Nations members sent troops to support South Korea. Soon, North Korea was forced to retreat. Then, President Truman and the UN decided to invade North Korea, hoping to reunite the two halves of Korea.

3. **DRAW YOUR ANSWER** Draw a simple map that shows how Korea was split in 1945 and the type of government in each half.

The war ends in stalemate

Communist China felt threatened by UN forces in North Korea. In November 1950, China attacked and drove the UN troops back into South Korea. The war ended with a cease-fire. No side had won a clear victory.

Cold War tensions continue

Former general Dwight D. Eisenhower followed Harry Truman as president. Eisenhower's secretary of state, John Foster Dulles, announced a policy tougher than containment. The United States would go to the brink of war to fight communism. This approach was known as brinksmanship.

4. In your own words, explain the main difference between brinksmanship and containment.

_____

_____

_____

LOOk CLOser

Europe after World War II, 1955

Member of NATO, 1955
Member of Warsaw Pact, 1955
Neutral country, 1955

0 150 300 miles
0 150 300 kilometers
Lambert Azimuthal Equal-Area Projection

✐ Mark It Up!

5. This map shows European nations that formed alliances after World War II. It also shows nations that remained neutral.
   • **Write** the letter *W* on the nations that were members of the Warsaw Pact.
   • **Circle** the names of the nations that were members of NATO.
   • **Write** the letter *N* on the nations that remained neutral.

Copyright © by McDougal Littell, a division of Houghton Mifflin Company

SECTION
2

The Vietnam War

For use with pages 538–542

Before, You Learned

After World War II, U.S. efforts to stop communism's spread included involvement in the Korean War.

Now You Will Learn

In the 1960s, the United States fought against communism in Vietnam.

Preview Terms & Names

- **Ho Chi Minh:** Communist leader of North Vietnam after World War II
- **Viet Cong:** Communist rebel group in South Vietnam
- **Gulf of Tonkin Resolution:** 1964 law that gave the U.S. president the power to use military force in Vietnam
- **Tet offensive:** major Viet Cong attack that became the turning point of the war

Take Notes as You Read

1.

CATEGORIZING	
Reasons for U.S. Involvement in Vietnam	**Reasons against U.S. Involvement in Vietnam**
France • The United States supported France regaining control of Vietnam.	**Progress of the war** •
Communism •	**South Vietnamese civilians** •

The United States aids the French

Vietnam is a country in Southeast Asia. It was a French colony, but it was occupied by Japan during World War II. After the war, Communist leader Ho Chi Minh declared Vietnam's independence from France. France, however, wanted to regain control of its colony.

In 1946, war broke out between France and Vietnam. U.S. leaders agreed to help France because they did not want Vietnam to become Communist. They feared that if Vietnam became Communist, the rest of Southeast Asia would follow. Also, the U.S. leaders wanted France's support in the struggle against the Soviets.

Dividing the North and the South

In 1954, France and Vietnam signed a peace agreement called the Geneva Accords. It split Vietnam into two countries. Ho Chi Minh ruled North Vietnam. Anticommunist Ngo Dinh Diem ruled South Vietnam, with U.S. support. Elections to reunify the country were set for 1956. But Diem refused to hold them. He feared that Communists would win and rule all of Vietnam.

2. In your own words, explain why France had U.S. support in its war with Vietnam.

_____

_____

_____

CHAPTER 24

The Viet Cong oppose Diem

Diem was a harsh, corrupt leader, and he did not establish a democratic government, as promised. A Communist rebel group known as the Viet Cong tried to overthrow Diem. North Vietnam sent soldiers and supplies to the Viet Cong on a path called the Ho Chi Minh Trail. In response, the U.S. gave more support to South Vietnam.

Johnson sends combat troops

In 1964, President Johnson asked Congress to pass the Gulf of Tonkin Resolution. This law gave the president the power to use military force in Vietnam. In March 1965, Johnson sent the first U.S. troops to Vietnam. By the end of 1968, more than 536,000 U.S. troops were involved.

3. **DRAW YOUR ANSWER** Draw a symbol that represents the Ho Chi Minh Trail.

A frustrating war; The Tet offensive

Many Americans thought the United States would quickly defeat the Viet Cong, but the war was difficult. One reason was that U.S. soldiers were young and inexperienced. Another was that the Viet Cong used surprise attacks called guerrilla warfare. In addition, the people of South Vietnam did not support U.S. troops because their methods harmed many civilians.

In January 1968, the Communists launched a surprise attack on U.S. troops called the Tet offensive. It was a military defeat for the Communists, but it showed that the war would not end soon. After the Tet offensive, Johnson refused to send more troops to Vietnam and planned to work for peace.

4. In your own words, explain how the Tet offensive changed Johnson's war policy.

_____

_____

LOOk Closer

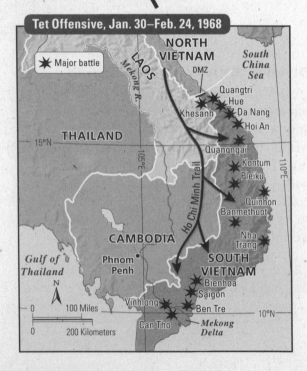

Tet Offensive, Jan. 30–Feb. 24, 1968

★ Major battle

NORTH VIETNAM
South China Sea
LAOS
Mekong R.
DMZ
Quangtri
Hue
Khesanh
Da Nang
Hoi An
THAILAND
15°N
105°E
Quangngai
Kontum
Ho Chi Minh Trail
Pleiku
110°E
Quinhon
Banmethuot
CAMBODIA
Nha Trang
Gulf of Thailand
Phnom Penh
SOUTH VIETNAM
N
Bienhoa
Saigon
0   100 Miles
Vinhlong
Ben Tre
10°N
0   200 Kilometers
Can Tho
Mekong Delta

✎ Mark It Up!

5. This map shows major battles that occurred during the Tet offensive.
   - **How** many major battles took place during the Tet offensive?

   _____

   - **Circle** the locations where the Ho Chi Minh Trail crossed into South Vietnam.
   - **Underline** the names of the two countries that border North and South Vietnam.

   _____

   _____

Name _____   Date _____

SECTION 3   # The Vietnam War Ends
For use with pages 543–547

Before, You Learned
In the 1960s, the United States fought against communism in Vietnam.

Now You Will Learn
As the United States began to end its involvement in Vietnam, the war deeply divided Americans.

Preview Terms & Names

- **doves:** opponents of the Vietnam War
- **hawks:** supporters of the Vietnam War
- **Richard Nixon:** elected president in 1968
- **Vietnamization:** Nixon's plan to slowly withdraw U.S. troops from Vietnam
- **War Powers Act:** 1973 law limiting the U.S. president's war-making powers

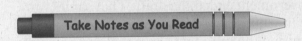
Take Notes as You Read

1.

CATEGORIZING	
Causes of Antiwar Feelings	**Effects of the Vietnam War**
U.S. draft •	**Vietnam** •
Bombing of Cambodia • Many Americans protested against Nixon's secret bombing raids.	**United States** •

A growing antiwar movement

As the war grew bloodier in the mid-1960s, antiwar feeling grew among Americans. Opinions opposing the war included these:

- The United States should not be involved in a foreign civil war.
- U.S. methods were immoral.
- The cost to America was too high.

Many young people protested the draft, which forced young men to serve in the military. They believed the draft unfairly targeted poor men and African Americans. People who opposed the war were called doves, while those who supported it were known as hawks.

1968—A turning point

The Tet offensive in January 1968 made Americans doubt the war could be won. Many Americans wanted U.S. troops to be withdrawn from Vietnam.

That summer, antiwar protesters were beaten by police outside the Democratic National Convention in Chicago. The chaos helped Republican candidate Richard Nixon win the presidency in 1968. He promised to bring "an honorable end to the war."

2. Why was 1968 a turning point in the war?

_____

_____

CHAPTER 24

Nixon's Vietnam strategy

In July 1969, Nixon announced his strategy of Vietnamization. He planned to slowly withdraw U.S. troops from South Vietnam. However, Nixon had begun secretly bombing Cambodia to stop Vietnamese use of Ho Chi Minh Trail. Public anger and distrust grew when Americans learned about the bombing raids.

U.S. withdrawal from Vietnam

Nixon was reelected in 1972. In January 1973, the United States and South Vietnam signed a peace agreement with North Vietnam. All U.S. troops withdrew. But North Vietnam broke the treaty in 1975 with its invasion of South Vietnam. The country was reunited with the Communists in control.

3. **DRAW YOUR ANSWER** Draw a symbol that represents Vietnam in 1975.

Legacy of the Vietnam War

The Vietnam War caused terrible destruction and suffering in Southeast Asia. It also took a heavy toll on U.S. soldiers. Many who survived suffered from injuries and stress-related problems. Also, once they arrived home, the public treated them coldly.

The war's political effects

The Vietnam War brought important political changes to the United States. In 1971, the Twenty-Sixth Amendment lowered the voting age from 21 to 18. In 1973, the government ended the draft. That same year, Congress passed the War Powers Act, limiting the president's war-making powers.

4. In your own words, explain two political effects of the Vietnam War on the U.S.

_____

_____

_____

LOOk Closer

✎ Mark It Up!

5. This image shows a pro-war rally in New York in 1970 and an antiwar rally in Washington in 1969.
   - **Write** the letter *P* on the side of the image that shows the pro-war rally.
   - **Write** the letter *A* on the side of the image that shows the antiwar rally.
   - **Write** a descriptive title for this image.

_____

Copyright © by McDougal Littell, a division of Houghton Mifflin Company

Name _____ Date _____

SECTION
4

The End of the Cold War
For use with pages 548–551

Before, You Learned
As the United States began to end its involvement in Vietnam, the war deeply divided Americans.

Now You Will Learn
During the 1980s, communism ended in the Soviet Union and Eastern Europe, ending the Cold War.

Preview Terms & Names

- **Ronald Reagan:** elected president in 1980
- **Mikhail Gorbachev:** became leader of the Soviet Union in 1985
- *glasnost:* name for Gorbachev's policy of greater openness in Soviet society
- **Solidarity:** Polish trade union that led a freedom movement against communism

Take Notes as You Read

1.

CATEGORIZING		
Communism after 1980		
East Germany	**Soviet Union**	**China**
•	•	• crushed protests for democracy in 1989
•	•	• remains Communist today

Gorbachev initiates reform
In 1985, Mikhail Gorbachev became the leader of the Soviet Union. He began many reforms to repair the ruined Soviet economy. He used a policy called *glasnost* to allow for greater freedoms in Soviet society.

Gorbachev also cut military spending and had a series of arms-control meetings with U.S. President Ronald Reagan.

The Americans and the Soviets agreed to eliminate two types of nuclear weapons. They also agreed to allow inspections of each other's military installations.

Communism ends in Eastern Europe
Gorbachev's actions caused people in other Communist countries to seek freedom. In Poland, Solidarity held large-scale strikes that forced the government to let noncommunists run in elections.

In October 1989, East Germans held massive protests against their Communist government. On November 9, 1989, East Germany opened the Berlin Wall. East and West Germany were reunited in 1990.

2. Explain how Germany changed in 1990.

_____

CHAPTER 24

The Soviet Union collapses

Next, people in the Soviet Union began to fight for their freedom. Individual republics declared their independence. In 1991, Gorbachev resigned, and the Soviet Union was no more. The Cold War was over.

3. In your own words, explain how the Cold War ended.

_____

_____

Communism continues in China

In the early 1980s, Communist China gave more freedom to businesses. Citizens then began to call for more political freedoms.

In April 1989, Chinese university students held a large demonstration in Tiananmen Square. China's ruler, Li Peng, ordered the military to crush the protesters, and many unarmed students were killed.

The world's democracies criticized Peng's response. Today, China's Communist rulers struggle to maintain political control while increasing economic freedom. China has become a world leader in trade.

The world's lone superpower

The United States has become the world's only global superpower. As a result, the United States gets involved in conflicts across the world to help keep the peace and restore order to war-torn regions.

Americans are divided over the nation's role in foreign conflicts. Some believe the U.S. has a responsibility to less powerful nations. Others believe the U.S. should stay out of other countries' conflicts.

4. **DRAW YOUR ANSWER** Draw a symbol that represents America's role as a world superpower.

LOOk Closer

Mark It Up!

5. This image shows protesters at the Berlin Wall.
   - **Reread** the section titled "Communism ends in Eastern Europe."
   - **Was** the Berlin Wall located in East Germany or West Germany?

   _____

   - **When** was the Berlin Wall finally opened?

   _____

SECTION
1

Political Developments in North Carolina

For use with pages 557–561

Before, You Learned

To stop the spread of communism, the United States went to war in Korea and Vietnam.

Now You Will Learn

The Republican Party and the U.S. military have influenced North Carolina politics.

Preview Terms & Names

- **incumbent:** an official who holds a political office while seeking reelection
- **delegation:** a group of official representatives
- **Jesse Helms:** Republican senator from North Carolina who served five terms in Congress

Take Notes as You Read

1.

FINDING SUPPORTING DETAILS	
Main Idea	**Supporting Details**
The Republican Party has gained strength in North Carolina since the 1970s.	
The military is an important force in North Carolina's politics.	

Republicans gain strength in state government

The Republican Party gained strength in North Carolina throughout the second half of the twentieth century.

In 1977, the state constitution was amended. The amendment states that governors can serve two consecutive four-year terms and an unlimited number of nonconsecutive terms. As a result, Democrat James B. Hunt, Jr., served as governor from 1977 to 1985, and then again from 1993 to 2001. A Republican, James Martin, also served as governor for eight years. Before the amendment, governors could serve only one four-year term.

The new governor; Judicial elections

Democrat Michael F. Easley was elected governor in 2000. That same year, Democrats were also elected to top positions in the state government. Easley was reelected in 2004.

In 2000, however, Republicans won more judgeships than Democrats. A Republican justice defeated the Democratic incumbent for chief justice of the Supreme Court.

2. How did Democrats and Republicans succeed in the 2000 state elections?

_____

_____

CHAPTER 25

Congressional seats

The 2000 elections did not change North Carolina's delegation to the House of Representatives. All 12 incumbents were reelected. Because North Carolina's population had grown, the state gained a thirteenth House seat in 2002.

In 2000, there was no change in the state's U.S. Senate representation because neither was up for reelection. Jesse Helms, who had served five terms in Congress, was responsible for the growth of the Republican Party in North Carolina. He did not run for reelection in 2002.

3. DRAW YOUR ANSWER Draw a picture that represents North Carolina's delegation to the House of Representatives in the 2000 election.

Presidential politics in North Carolina

Elizabeth Dole was elected as senator in 2002. In 2004, John Edwards left his Senate seat to run for president. Republican Richard Burr took his place.

Since 1972, the Republican presidential has won North Carolina's electoral votes in all but one election. In 2004, presidential candidate John Kerry picked Edwards to run as his vice-presidential candidate. Nevertheless, North Carolina backed Republican George W. Bush.

Military bases in North Carolina

North Carolina has seven military bases. These bases play a crucial role in the defense of American interests at home and abroad.

4. Why was the 2004 presidential election unusual for North Carolina?

_____

_____

_____

L👁👁k Cl⊕ser

Military Bases in North Carolina

✎ Mark It Up!

5. This map shows the seven U.S. military bases located in North Carolina.

- **Circle** North Carolina's two U.S. Air Force Bases.
- **Underline** the name of North Carolina's U.S. Coast Guard station.
- **Draw** an arrow to the military base located closest to the city of Havelock.

Copyright © by McDougal Littell, a division of Houghton Mifflin Company

SECTION 2
Economic and Environmental Issues
For use with pages 562–566

Before, You Learned
The Republican Party and the U.S. military have influenced North Carolina politics.

Now You Will Learn
The state's economy has been challenged by a decline in manufacturing, but energized by new industries.

Preview Terms & Names

- **gross state product:** the total value of goods and services produced in a state in a year
- **globalization:** linking economies around the world
- **free trade:** removing trade barriers to help link economies
- **biotechnology:** the use of living cells and organisms to help create medicines, vaccines, and better foods

Take Notes as You Read

1.

FINDING SUPPORTING DETAILS	
Main Idea North Carolina's economy faces challenges.	**Supporting Details**
North Carolina has new economic opportunities.	

Preparing for the future; Assessing people's needs

In 1981, Governor James B. Hunt, Jr., created the Commission on the Future of North Carolina to help the state face future challenges. The commission made several recommendations:

- Education: supporting schools, training teachers, and offering daycare
- Health: protecting workers, increasing health care, and improving public education
- Housing: more affordable housing
- Poverty: providing job training to women and minority groups

- Business: improving public transportation, finding new energy sources, and creating new communication networks

Modern changes and challenges

Through most of the 1990s, the state's economy grew. This growth had slowed by 2001, partly due to damages from Hurricane Floyd, falling farm prices, and a nationwide recession.

2. Explain the purpose of the Commission on the Future of North Carolina.

_____

_____

CHAPTER 25

Changing conditions in agriculture

North Carolina is a national leader in the production of hogs, chickens, cotton, and soybeans. However, prices for these products have fallen. In response, farmers have begun growing different crops and using technology to make their farms more productive.

The challenges of globalization

Manufacturing provides about one-fourth of North Carolina's gross state product. In 2001, the state's manufacturing industry entered a recession.

Some believe this recession is due to globalization, or the linking of economies around the world. A key part of globalization is free trade, or removing trade barriers to link economies among nations.

3. What does the term *free trade* mean?

_____

_____

The debate over NAFTA

The North American Free Trade Agreement promotes trade between the United States, Canada, and Mexico. Some people believe NAFTA led to the loss of manufacturing jobs in North Carolina.

New industries emerge

North Carolina's Research Triangle Park has brought high-tech jobs to the state, such as biotechnology, information technology, and filmmaking.

Protecting the environment

North Carolina's economic growth has raised concerns about the impact on the environment. State leaders have passed laws to protect the environment.

4. **DRAW YOUR ANSWER** Draw a symbol that represents the purpose of NAFTA.

LOOk Cl⊕ser

PRIMARY SOURCE

Our task today is to anticipate and prepare for the North Carolina our children will encounter tomorrow. . . . We must take responsibility for making the world what we want it to be, for ourselves and for our children. And that requires looking into the future now. Looking at the future can help us anticipate changes and make decisions. It can help prepare us for what lies ahead and put us in the driver's seat, to chart the course for North Carolina.

Governor James B. Hunt, Jr.

Mark It Up!

5. This quotation is from Governor Hunt's "Speech on Commission on the Future of North Carolina."
   - **Underline** the main responsibilities of the commission.
   - **Circle** two benefits that Hunt says will come from looking into the future.

Copyright © by McDougal Littell, a division of Houghton Mifflin Company

SECTION
3 North Carolina's People and Culture
For use with pages 567–571

Before, You Learned
North Carolina's economy has been challenged.

Now You Will Learn
Rapid population growth between 1950 and 2000 led to changes in North Carolina's culture and society.

Preview Terms & Names

- **natural increase:** an increase in population that is the result of more births than deaths
- **demographer:** a scientist who studies population statistics

Take Notes as You Read

1.

FINDING SUPPORTING DETAILS

Main Idea	Supporting Details
North Carolina's population is growing and becoming more diverse.	
The arts and sports are important parts of North Carolina's culture.	

Population growth and distribution
Between 1950 and 2000, North Carolina's population nearly doubled. Reasons for the increase included natural increase, or more births than deaths, and migration from other states and other countries.

Job opportunities and the moderate climate attracted more than a half million newcomers in the 1990s. In addition, officials estimate that thousands of immigrants entered the state illegally. This means they did not have proper immigration documents.

Ethnic diversity
North Carolina's population increasingly includes people of different cultures and ethnicities. The Asian segment has grown by 118 percent. Hispanics are one of the largest minority groups in the state.

Hispanic culture, from food to music, can be found in many areas. Schools have faced the challenge of educating large numbers of Hispanic students for whom English is not their native language.

2. In your own words, explain North Carolina's population growth.

_____

_____

CHAPTER 25

CHAPTER 25

Consequences of rapid population growth

Demographers are scientists who study population statistics. They predict that North Carolina's population will continue to grow. The increased population will need more:

- vehicles, which will crowd roads and increase pollution;
- housing and shopping areas;
- doctors and health care facilities, especially for the aging population; and
- teachers and schools.

A rich culture; A tradition of sports

North Carolina has many successful art, music, and theater programs. The North Carolina Symphony is the first state-funded symphony, and the North Carolina School of the Arts is one of the finest performing arts schools in the world.

The state has long been known for its excellent college basketball teams. In recent years, North Carolina has become home to a number of professional sports teams, which is another sign of the state's growth.

Civic participation

North Carolina is home to a number of groups committed to causes, such as protecting the environment and increasing civic awareness.

- Kids Voting North Carolina educates young people about civic participation.
- The Collegiate Recyclers Coalition promotes recycling on college campuses.

3. In your own words, explain the main purpose of Kids Voting North Carolina.

_____

_____

_____

LOOk Closer

Population of North Carolina, 1950–2005

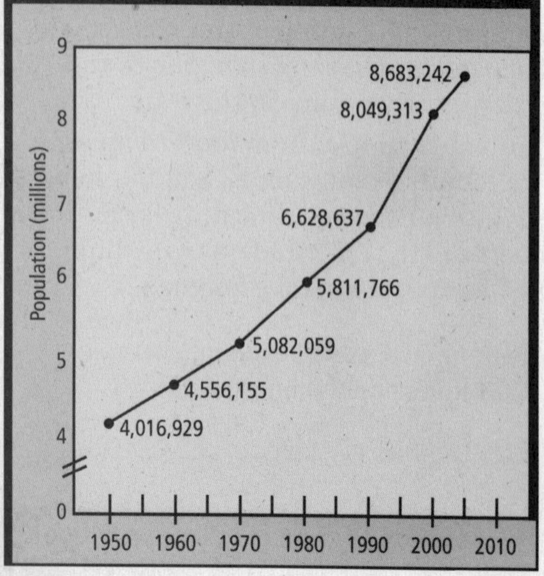

Mark It Up!

4. This chart shows North Carolina's population growth from 1950 to 2005.
   - **Circle** the year when North Carolina's population reached about 8 million.
   - **Calculate** how many more people lived in North Carolina in 2005 than in 1950.

_____

Copyright © by McDougal Littell, a division of Houghton Mifflin Company

SECTION
4

North Carolina and Global Issues

For use with pages 572–575

Before, You Learned

Rapid population growth led to changes in North Carolina's culture and society.

Now You Will Learn

A number of global events have touched the United States and North Carolina.

Preview Terms & Names

- **Camp David Accords:** peace agreement between Israel and Egypt brokered by President Carter in 1979
- **terrorism:** the use or threatened use of violence for political or social reasons
- **Saddam Hussein:** former leader of Iraq who was removed from power in 2003

Take Notes as You Read

1.

FINDING SUPPORTING DETAILS	
Main Idea The U.S. has tried to help bring peace to the Middle East.	**Supporting Details**
The U.S. has become involved in military action against countries in the Middle East.	

Turmoil in the Middle East

Most Middle Eastern nations are home to Arabs, people who speak the Arabic language. However, most people in Iran are Persians and speak the Persian language.

Most Arabs and Iranians are Muslims, people who follow the religion of Islam. Israel is also part of the Middle East. Most Israelis practice the Jewish religion. The Middle East is rich in oil deposits and many nations, including the United States, have taken a great interest in the region.

Over the past 40 years, the Middle East has experienced a lot of conflict. Much of the conflict has been caused by hatred between Israel and its Arab neighbors.

U.S. efforts at peace

There have been many attempts to bring peace to the Middle East. In 1978, President Jimmy Carter brought the leaders of Egypt and Israel together at Camp David in Maryland.

The leaders signed a peace agreement known as the Camp David Accords. It was the first signed agreement between Israel and an Arab country. However, conflict continued.

2. What were the Camp David Accords?

_____

_____

CHAPTER 25

September 11, 2001

On September 11, 2001, the United States was the target of terrorism, the use or threatened use of violence for political or social reasons. Approximately 3,000 people died from the attacks, which were blamed on terrorist Osama Bin Laden and the group al-Qaeda.

President Bush vowed to hunt down those responsible and to eliminate all forms of terrorism. Troops from North Carolina were among the first to be sent to Afghanistan to hunt for Osama Bin Laden.

3. In your own words, explain how North Carolina was involved in the war with Afghanistan.

_____

_____

The war in Iraq; The struggle continues

In 2003, the United States turned its attention to Iraq and its leader, Saddam Hussein. U.S. leaders were concerned that Hussein had weapons of mass destruction.

U.S. and British forces invaded Iraq in March 2003. Hussein was captured, put on trial, and later hanged for his crimes.

Afterward, U.S. troops stayed in Iraq to battle resistance fighters. Americans became divided over the war, particularly when no weapons of mass destruction were found.

North Carolina looks forward

Amid war and other global concerns, North Carolina looks ahead. The state's businesses, industries, and universities will help it succeed in the future.

4. **DRAW YOUR ANSWER** Draw a picture that represents the war in Iraq.

LO0k Cl◉ser

🖉 Mark It Up!

5. This photograph shows (from left to right) President Anwar el-Sadat of Egypt, President Carter, and Prime Minister Menachem Begin of Israel at the signing of the Camp David Accords in 1979.
   • **Write** three words that describe the action shown in the photograph.

_____

_____

_____